DIRECTING WEB TRAFFIC

Philip Smith

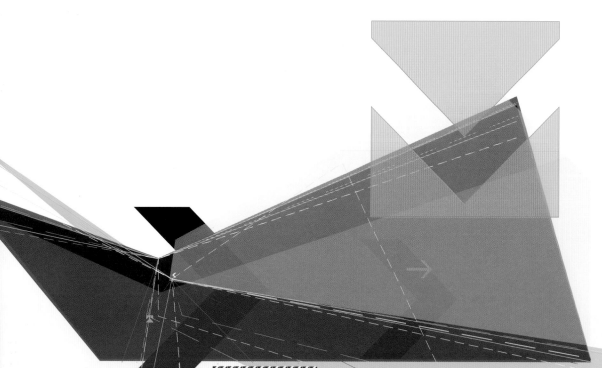

A RotoVision Book
Published and distributed
by RotoVision SA
Route Suisse 9
CH-1295 Mies
Switzerland

RotoVision SA
Sales, Editorial & Production Office
Sheridan House
112/116A Western Road
Hove, East Sussex BN3 1DD, UK
Tel: +44 (0)1273 72 72 68
Fax: +44 (0)1273 72 72 69
Email: sales@rotovision.com
www.rotovision.com

[author: philip smith]

DESIGNED & ILLUSTRATED BY **bark**   email bark@barkdesign.demon.co.uk
www.barkdesign.demon.co.uk

10 9 8 7 6 5 4 3 2 1
ISBN 2-88046-701-2

Production and separations
by ProVision Pte. Ltd. in Singapore
Tel: +65 334 7720
Fax: +65 334 7721

Although every effort has been made to contact owners of copyright material reproduced in
this book, we have not always been successful. In the event of a copyright query, please
contact the publisher.

DIRECTING WEB TRAFFIC

RotoVision

DIRECTING WEB TRAFFIC

CONTENTS

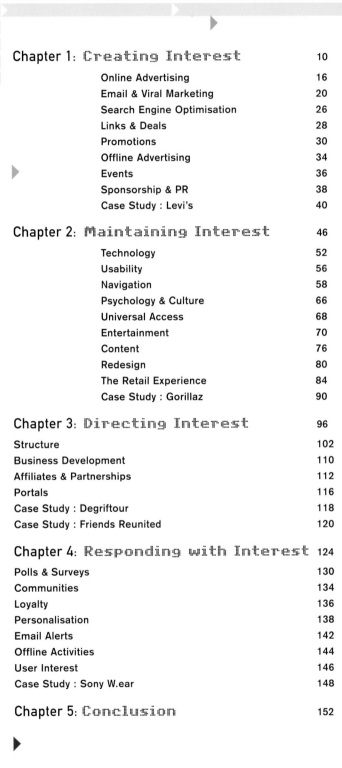

[dobedo.se] The Swedish community web site Dobedo used animated avatars of each user to allow people to interact online.

[amazon.com] Amazon's web site is still regarded as an e-tail classic for its design simplicity and use of innovations like personalisation and email marketing

[Heavy.com] The American entertainment and music web site Heavy.com relies on its users spending a long time interacting with the site. Hence the emphasis on rich media and the range of services it provides on the home page.

[habbohotel.co.uk] Aimed at teenagers, Habbo Hotel is another avatar-based community site but its design is affected by the opportunities it offers for advertising and sponsorship.

INTRODUCTION

Just like it is no longer good enough to say that you want to build a web site because everyone else is, whether it be for yourself or your multi-national corporate employer, it is no longer good enough to leave the design and appearance of the site as an afterthought. The success or failure of any online venture depends on its design. A web site is not solely about technology and the environment that spawned it, it is about how that technology — both software and hardware — is put to use.

As ideas and businesses have spawned, thrived, and, of course, in many cases failed on the Internet over the last few years, the appreciation of design and a clarity of purpose as central to the success or otherwise of any new media venture has grown. The design of a web site is integral to fulfilling its ambitions successfully. The continued simplicity of Amazon's home page has contributed immensely to the e-tailer's global success. Sites built around content and 'stickiness', or the ability to retain users' attention, can only succeed if the design facilitates their aims and allows the user to fulfill those aims with clear instructions or instinctive operation.

The failure of dotcoms like the highly ambitious global sportswear e-tailer boo.com was due in no small part to the design and layout of the site and the reliance of that design on unreliable technology and software. The delivery failed to live up to the promise of the appearance.

Simplicity is not a prerequisite for every type of online design, of course. After all, having the best levels of customer service in the world and a superslick fulfilment operation can only be effective if customers are engaged by the site in the first place — and different users look for different things. Not only should a site developer bear the needs of the audience in mind, but also what the objective of

the site is. Also those sites that have endured, or are entering the market for the first time now, are finding that a new breed of user — which is getting more sophisticated as it understands more about a maturing medium — has different expectations and different demands. In that case, design needs to be enduring but flexible.

Certainly, first impressions do last, and the hard-to-find and obscure 'Buy Now' button has put off many first time purchasers. Let alone, the negative effect that an annoying virtual shopping assistant that refuses to load onto users' screens properly can have.

The online world is effectively a self-service place where the customer can easily leave his or her trolley in the aisle on the way to the checkout at any stage without the embarrassment of walking out of a shop mid-way through a transaction. Online snobbery will never cut it — the retailer or marketer or any other form of online media owner must make each and every visitor feel welcome so that those valuable eyeballs come back soon to look or buy - or whatever you want them to do - on your site. So ease of use is paramount and the rise and rise of the appreciation of online design disciplines like usability and their role in the development process of a site only underlines the fact. The case of universal access — most obviously taking into account the needs of the blind and partially sighted — is another factor. Particularly now that a range of countries and communities like the EU have taken steps to make this a regulatory issue.

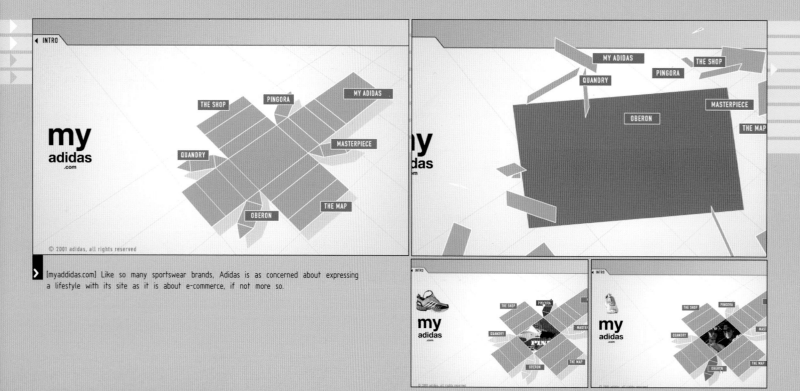

INTRODUCTION

First impressions count, but, of course, they are only a part of the story. Designers should take into account where they want their web site users and viewers to go next. And whether they want them to return.

This spreads into the marketing arena as marketeers have become more and more keen to exploit digital channels as medium to bring potential customers and visitors back to their online businesses. This does not preclude the use of offline advertising, in the broadcast, print and outdoor arenas – as some of the most successful companies have found out   by running truly integrated marketing initiatives.

Online marketing tactics and ideas which have become accepted range from affiliate marketing relationships to the more straightforward specialism of internet advertising and the range of formats offered by online media-owners. From the basic banner-ad to the more complex

rich-media formats such as Superstitial adverts, advertising creative has been asked to do more and pushed further to make an impact and this has given designers even more challenges.Concepts such as viral marketing have thrived online as the idea of selling an idea by word-of-mouth has proved more cost-effective than traditional marketing concepts when exploited by a range of brands and online businesses. Again, the best of such executions place new and specific demands on the designer.

The fastest-growing medium in history continues to evolve; the pace of change is bewildering. But the best of the new breed of online businesses, brand owners and web designers are adapting to those changes, using a variety of techniques from the visual to the commercial to ensure that users still visit, enjoy and return to their sites.

[la planete des singes] Film companies and fans have embraced the web as a marketing medium as seen by this French site for the Tim Burton film Planet of the Apes.

CREATING INTEREST

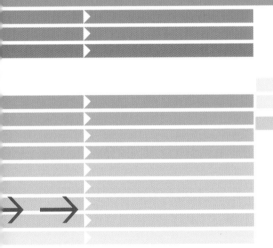

11

CREATING INTEREST **INTRODUCTION**

So there are all those people out there, potential viewers, users and customers of every web site, and more and more of them are coming online everyday. According to surveyors Nielsen//NetRatings, by the third quarter of 2001 some 474 million people had Internet access at home.

Ultimately, there are two basic sources of viewers – or eyeballs, as online advertisers and media-owners know them: they can be established and regular web users who have made their online debut long ago, or they can be Internet novices who have to be 'lured' online with the promise of entertainment, cost savings or some other incentive which businesses, advertisers and marketers have endeavoured to do mainly by using offline channels, from posterboards to print advertising to TV commercials.

The difference, of course, is that the online business advertising offline not only has to attract people's attention and sell the virtues of a site, but it often has to explain the properties of the Internet as a medium. However, this should become less and less a consideration as the web becomes an increasingly common part of everyday life. Many web marketeers will heave a sign of relief as that becomes more

and more apparent. Dotcom horror stories revolve around misplaced marketing spend and the perception that several business plans for online-only businesses consisted of little more than spending money on high-profile offline marketing campaigns, with logos adorning everything in the non-virtual world from taxis to billboards, creating little more than confusion in the general public.

Basic mistakes include launching the offline campaign before there is a fully functioning web site to direct potential customers to, as boo.com found out to its cost. The Swedish-based sportswear e-tailer kicked off its advertising campaign in cinemas and the style press some six months before its web site was launched. TV advertising by dotcoms has seen mixed results as well. British Internet Service Provider (ISP) breathe.net has attracted opprobrium for its hard-to-understand television campaign, run in an attempt to build a brand and through that its customer base. Centred around apparently everyday activities – as easy as breathing, it claimed – the campaign which first hit TV screens in 1999 was roundly criticised for not explaining what breathe was, let alone why viewers should be using the ISP, rather than, say, the UK's largest such business, Freeserve.

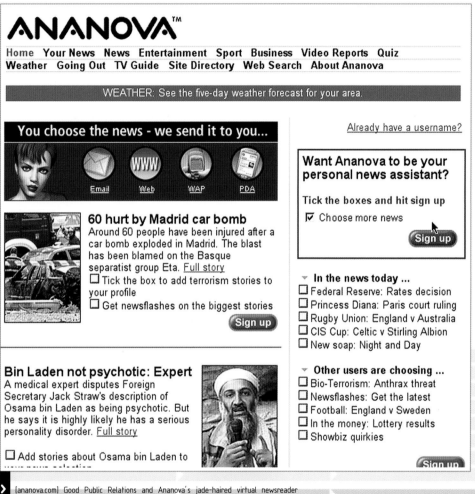

ANANOVA™

Home Your News News Entertainment Sport Business Video Reports Quiz
Weather Going Out TV Guide Site Directory Web Search About Ananova

WEATHER: See the five-day weather forecast for your area.

You choose the news - we send it to you...

Email   Web   WAP   PDA

60 hurt by Madrid car bomb
Around 60 people have been injured after a car bomb exploded in Madrid. The blast has been blamed on the Basque separatist group Eta. Full story
☐ Tick the box to add terrorism stories to your profile
☐ Get newsflashes on the biggest stories
Sign up

Bin Laden not psychotic: Expert
A medical expert disputes Foreign Secretary Jack Straw's description of Osama bin Laden as being psychotic. But he says it is highly likely he has a serious personality disorder. Full story

☐ Add stories about Osama bin Laden to

Already have a username?

Want Ananova to be your personal news assistant?

Tick the boxes and hit sign up
☑ Choose more news
Sign up

▾ **In the news today ...**
☐ Federal Reserve: Rates decision
☐ Princess Diana: Paris court ruling
☐ Rugby Union: England v Australia
☐ CIS Cup: Celtic v Stirling Albion
☐ New soap: Night and Day

▾ **Other users are choosing ...**
☐ Bio-Terrorism: Anthrax threat
☐ Newsflashes: Get the latest
☐ Football: England v Sweden
☐ In the money: Lottery results
☐ Showbiz quirkies

Sign up

[ananova.com] Good Public Relations and Ananova's jade-haired virtual newsreader gave the news web site plenty of helpful publicity when it launched.

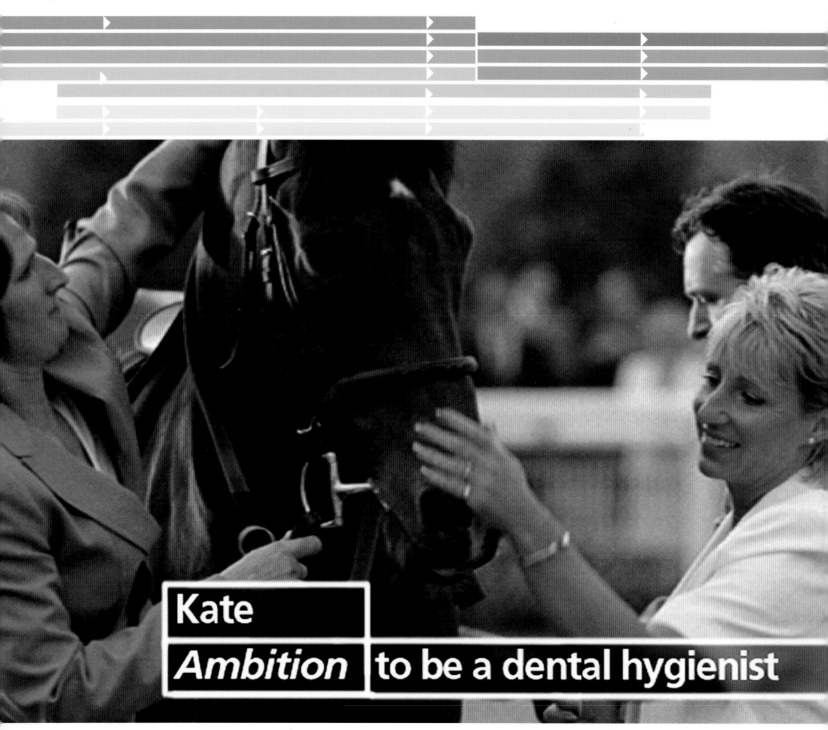

Kate

Ambition to be a dental hygienist

However, some web sites have stuck to their guns and continued to advertise offline. StepStone, the European recruitment site, for example, has continually sponsored sports programmes on TV. In the UK, teen site mykindaplace has linked up with broadcaster Sky to sponsor Buffy the Vampire Slayer. In the middle of 2001, ebookers, the travel site, even renounced online advertising in its marketing strategy and has vowed to build its business through offline marketing as it feels it needs to capture customer who may not be regular users of the Internet. Smaller-scale sites find advertising opportunities everywhere from specialist magazines to the bags that their target audience buy their lunchtime sandwiches in.

The second option for sites to pursue to build traffic is via the Internet itself. Not only have new marketing disciplines – such as search engine optimisation – been developed for the online arena, but also the Internet has breathed new life into direct marketing ideas and concepts such as word-of-mouth brand building and guerrilla marketing. According to a survey conducted by the online advertising specialist DoubleClick, around half of all European marketeers are using online marketing ideas and tools. In the UK, this has reached 73 per cent. Email marketing (see page 20) was the main format, with banner advertising (see page 16) the second most popular.

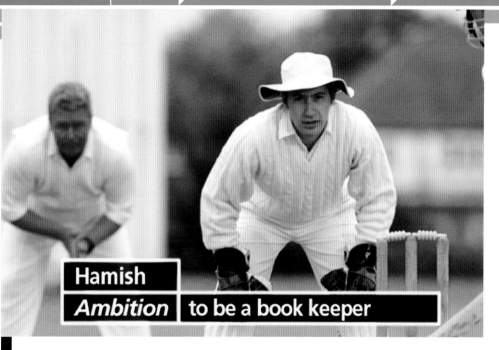

[StepStone TV advertising] Online recruitment company StepStone spent heavily in order to build its brand through offline advertising such as its sponsorship of TV sports programmes.

CREATING INTEREST ONLINE ADVERTISING

The Internet has created a variety of new advertising formats and media – banners, buttons, pop-ups, and Rich Media, including Superstitials and blipverts. According to the Interactive Advertising Bureau, the first banner advert on a site was sold in November 1994. The market is now worth an estimated £154 million a year in the UK alone – more than one per cent of the country's total advertising expenditure.

Since 1994, an entire industry has grown up around advertising online which encompasses everyone from the creative agencies which design the banner ads to media planners and buyers and specialist online advertising sales houses which sell ad space on sites and the networks which host them for the media owner.

This means that not only does the basic banner advertising shape – a rectangle traditionally running across the top of a web page in the centre – have an effect on a site's design, but online advertising as a whole has become more and more influential on the site's look as new advertising formats have been invented and approved. The IAB's definition of the basic unit of advertising online, the banner advertisement, is: 'An advertisement in the form of a graphic image that typically runs across a web page or is positioned in a margin or other space reserved for ads. The most

common larger banner ad is 468 pixels wide by 60 pixels high. Smaller sizes include 125 by 125 and 120 by 90 pixels. The Interactive Advertising Bureau (IAB) has established these and other banner sizes as standard sizes.'

However, despite some impressive growth rates in the value of online advertising, it has had its critics and problems. First, click-through rates (so-called because a user clicks on the banner advertisement to be directed to the advertiser's web site) have fallen, which has been blamed on users' increasing sophistication and familiarity with online advertising. This has led to bigger and more unusual ad spaces, such as the 120 x 600 Skyscraper format, which normally runs vertically along the right of the page, as the viewer looks at it.

This has coincided with media owners' insistence that click-through rates are not the only way of measuring the success of online advertising. It can be a brand building tool as well, used to maintain awareness of the advertiser's site, even if it does not drive traffic directly to it. However, this has its problems as well. In November 2001, a report from British media intelligence group Thomson Intermedia said that in a survey of UK users using its 20,000-strong consumer Internet panel, users find all forms of

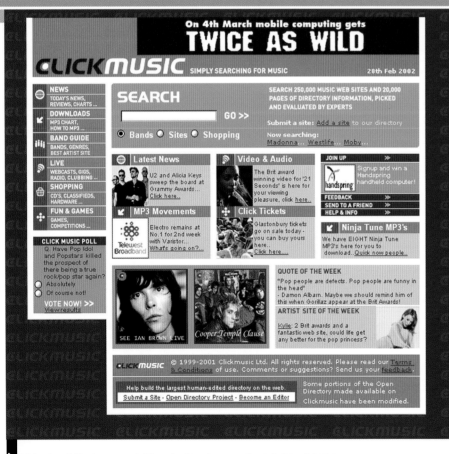

[clickmusic.com] The homepage of this music site makes a prominent feature of banner advertising.

Internet advertising to be irritating. Pop-ups are by far the most disliked. Interstitials (the ads that appear when a user tries to click through to a new page) come next in Thomson's survey. It says: 'The most important influences on whether a user will click on an ad are the content of the site advertised and special offers/promotions.' It concludes: 'Brand recognition and the design of the ad are much less influential but both of these are much more important to younger users.' Charles Ilsley, research director at Thomson Intermedia, says: 'We would expect similar user responses to banners, pop-ups and interstitials had we asked what people thought of TV or direct mail ads. This suggests that advertisers must be careful about exactly how they use more intrusive forms of advertising such as pop-ups and, to a lesser extent, interstitials.'

> [mediaguardian.co.uk] Media planning and buying is as important to an online advertising campaign as it is in traditional media. Media owners, such as mediaguardian.co.uk, can provider advertisers with data on their reach and user-base.

> [eyeblaster.com] Hollywood blockbusters Oceans Eleven and Moulin Rouge were promoted on the Eyeblaster ad platform with rich media executions.

17

CREATING INTEREST **ONLINE ADVERTISING**

Much of today's online advertising borrows the forms, and some of the attitude of 'guerrilla marketing' – the sort of promotion that aims to attract attention either by creating a stunt or spectacle, or by subverting or appropriating some existing medium. It is known as guerrilla marketing because it is often done without official permission, or sails close to the wind in terms of legality – for example, in projecting logos onto public buildings. In fact, much 'guerrilla' marketing today is perfectly legal and has permission from the owner of whichever property hosts the stunt, but maintains the character and appearance of a subversive, edgy marketing 'raid'. In recent years it has been a useful tool for many brands and businesses, both online and offline.

Offline, guerrilla messages are useful ways of attracting the public's attention in order to spread a brand message. In the US, for example, recruitment site HotJobs.com sent marketeers onto the streets of Seattle to stand on soapboxes and heckle bystanders and passers-by with 'inspirational' messages about the company and its web site. A key part of the campaign was the use of chalkboards, on which the public was asked to write something catchy and inspirational about themselves and their jobs, which was used in other marketing activity.

[NTL ad] Cable company NTL used new ad formats and technology to make it look like rugby players were kicking a ball through the screen.

18

[Levi's ad] Levi's got plenty of attention and plaudits for the cutting-edge use of the Flat Eric icon – star of its offline campaigns – as a figure which appeared on different web sites to direct traffic to Levis.com.

On the Internet, specific tools and situations are covered by the guerrilla concept, but perhaps the most useful idea is to see it as a blurring of the dividing line between advertising and editorial content on a web site. Often creatively executed it can be used to build a brand, but more often than not it is used to drag users through to a different web site.

Often such executions rely on new ad formats and technology, including rich media executions and such as dhtml (dynamic html) programs or even the transparent ad format, as developed by companies such as Tangozebra. Most importantly, they rely on a media owner or third party web site being willing to host the 'guerrilla' campaign.

One way in which site owners use genuine guerrilla tactics is the practice of using the community sections of other web sites – usually aimed at specific niches and interest groups – to promote their own site and business message. This is usually done without the knowledge or permission of the host site, most of whom object to such blatant self-promotion and will delete any postings or threads which cross the boundary. However, as this is often an unwritten rule of Internet etiquette, a sophisticated and subtle

approach can be undetected. Of course, it should not be so subtle that a potentially interested party will miss the message.

Music site peoplesound.com got members of its marketing team to visit online chat rooms anonymously and encourage users to visit a music-themed microsite, which runs a peoplesound-themed pop quiz and offers prizes. Its justification was that it would post such messages only in response to a request for information or a stated interest in a subject.

The big problem posed by such efforts is the fact that if caught, the site or company being promoted can be linked with underhand and manipulative tactics rather than with the brand values it aspires to.

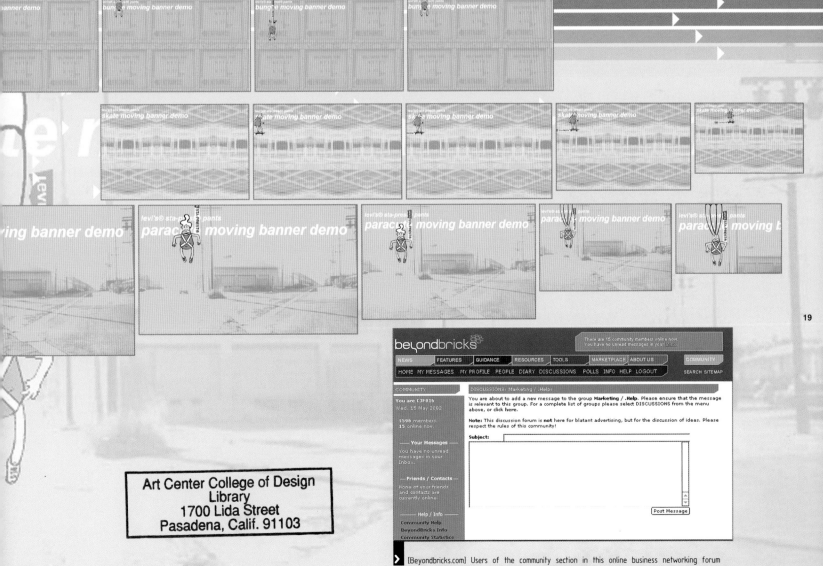

[Beyondbricks.com] Users of the community section in this online business networking forum are warned against posting ads for their own sites.

CREATING INTEREST EMAIL & VIRAL MARKETING

Email can be a powerful online marketing tool. Not only is it personal and can be directed straight to a user, but it is also cost-efficient. However, its success depends on the aims and ideas behind each use and campaign. Not only does the success of an emailing depend on the content of the message sent but it also depends on the database of recipients and how that has been acquired or collated.

There are, however, a number of innate advantages in using email. Perhaps most important, users are already online and through the use of links embedded in the email, they can be driven directly through to a web site or even a particular part of the web site, such as a particular news story on an information-driven content site.

Many organisations prefer to only send email to users that have requested information, or opted-in to a particular list, in order to prevent the risk of sending 'spam' or irrelevant email. Spam is particularly annoying – the online equivalent of junk mail – because of the personal nature of email; when we receive an email, we expect that it has been sent specifically to us and are annoyed to find that it is an advertisement for a product we do not want or a site we have no interest in. To have to visit that site merely to remove our names from the list of recipients compounds the annoyance.

Media intelligence group Thomson Intermedia found that almost three-quarters of its survey respondents are happy to get promotional emails from sites or companies with whom they have just registered. However, only 18 per cent are happy to get promotions by email from 'any' source; some eight per cent don't like to receive that form of email at all.

Frequency is another key point. Thomson found that just over 10 per cent of users are happy for companies to send them promotional emails every few days. Some 40 per cent would prefer to be mailed weekly, 20 per cent every two weeks and another 22 per cent monthly.

One increasingly popular form of marketing via email is viral marketing. The aim is to get the users themselves to do the marketing for the site by passing the email on to friends and – if truly effective – it will then be passed on to others by them. The advantage of viral marketing is fourfold: first, after the initial mailing, further dissemination of the message is free to the marketeer. Second, once the 'virus' is in circulation, the rate of spread is exponential – an email linked to the site of Turkish journalist Mahir Cagri, which users found funny, is reputed to have circulated the world in two days, resulting in over two million visits to the site. Third, those passing the email to friends have a much better idea than the marketeer about who is interested in what.

[lastminute.com] Travel and entertainment e-tailer lastminute.com has maintained a chatty and informal style in its emails to customers despite its growth into a multinational business.

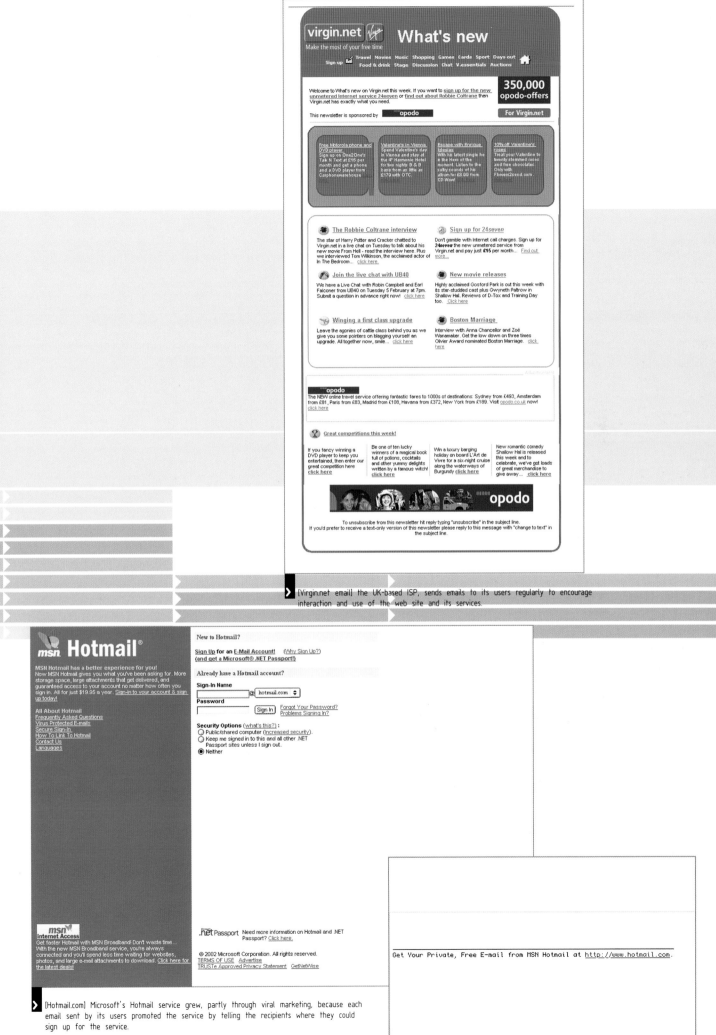

[Virgin.net email] the UK-based ISP, sends emails to its users regularly to encourage interaction and use of the web site and its services.

[Hotmail.com] Microsoft's Hotmail service grew, partly through viral marketing, because each email sent by its users promoted the service by telling the recipients where they could sign up for the service.

CREATING INTEREST EMAIL & VIRAL MARKETING

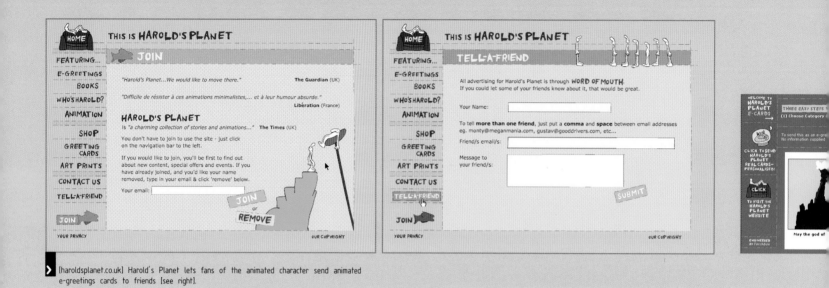

[haroldsplanet.co.uk] Harold's Planet lets fans of the animated character send animated e-greetings cards to friends [see right].

And fourth, the personal endorsement implied by passing on the email is extremely valuable. We are always more likely to trust and act on a recommendation from a friend than from advertising.

Many viral marketing campaigns involve jokes, cartoons or games – the type of material that friends are likely to want to exchange. Others, however, are more subtle: the success of Microsoft's Hotmail brand worldwide has often been attributed to viral marketing as each email sent by a user bears an advertisement for Hotmail at the bottom, and a link to the registration section of the site.

Many web sites today aim to capitalise on the potential of viral marketing by allowing users to alert friends to things on the site that they might find interesting – either by sending the item directly to them in an email (which they may then forward to other people) or by sending them an alert email, via the site, which names the friend who thought they might be interested in the site. Cricket site topstumps.com, for example, allows users to send challenges to an online game to friends – a useful facility for users which also helps the site's owner to build an email database.

A subtle variation of this can be seen in the e-cards which sites allow users to send to friends, via the site, with a personal message. An email is usually sent to the recipient, telling them that a card is waiting for them at the site. Clicking on a link takes them directly to their card, but after viewing it, they may browse further around the site.

Not all email marketing is viral – much is targeted to an individual user who has registered a specific interest, or appears on a customer database or similar source – but some of the most effective email marketing is.

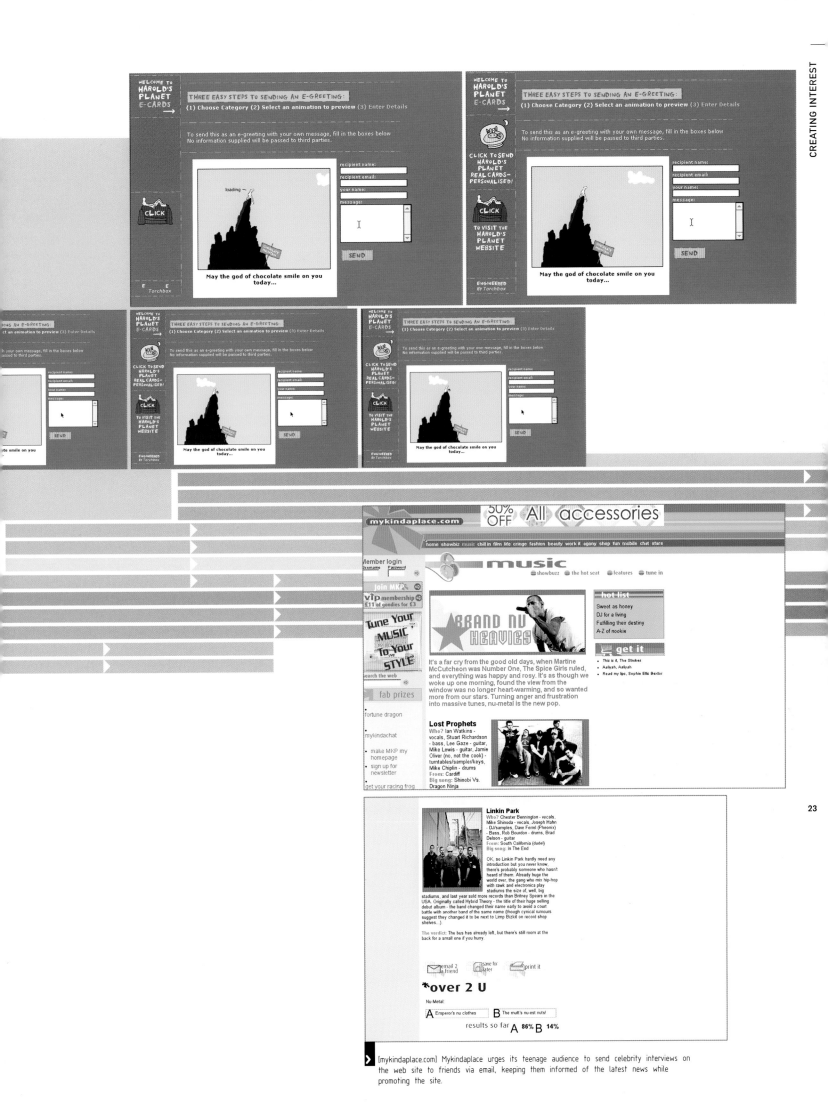

[mykindaplace.com] Mykindaplace urges its teenage audience to send celebrity interviews on the web site to friends via email, keeping them informed of the latest news while promoting the site.

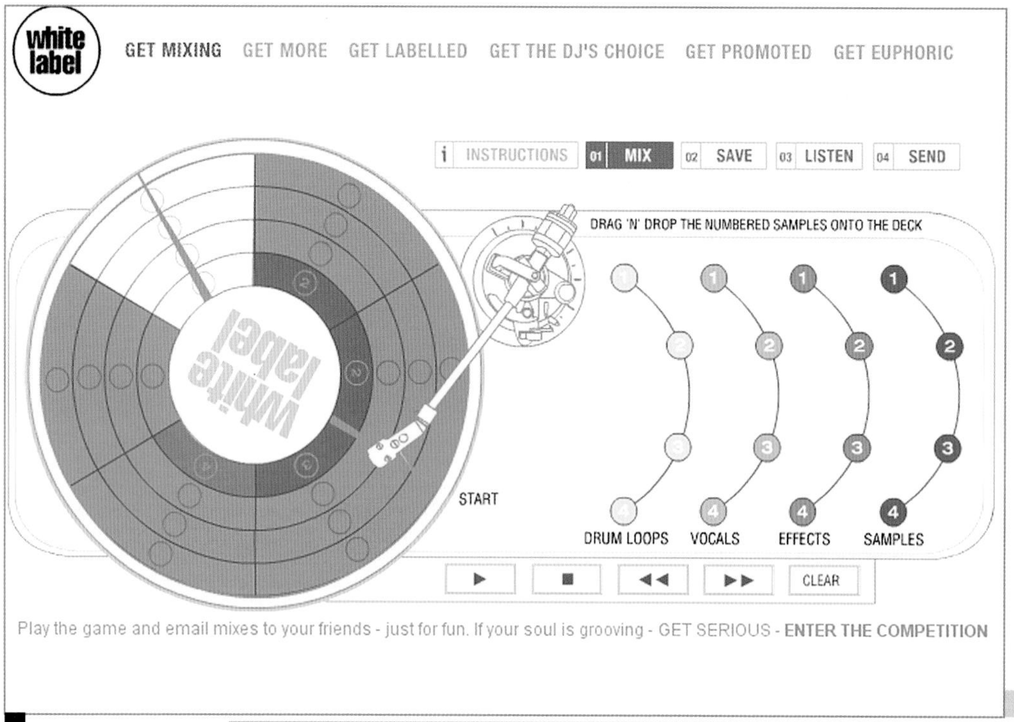

CREATING INTEREST **EMAIL & VIRAL MARKETING**

white label GET MIXING   GET MORE   GET LABELLED   GET THE DJ'S CHOICE   GET PROMOTED   GET EUPHORIC

ℹ INSTRUCTIONS 01 **MIX** 02 SAVE 03 LISTEN 04 SEND

DRAG 'N' DROP THE NUMBERED SAMPLES ONTO THE DECK

white label

START

DRUM LOOPS   VOCALS   EFFECTS   SAMPLES

▶ ■ ◀◀ ▶▶ CLEAR

Play the game and email mixes to your friends - just for fun. If your soul is grooving - GET SERIOUS - **ENTER THE COMPETITION**

> [lynxwhitelabel.com] The web allows people to interact with brands like the deodorant Lynx White Label in ways that they could not do before. This site asks them to mix their own music and send it to friends via the site, as well as enter a competition.

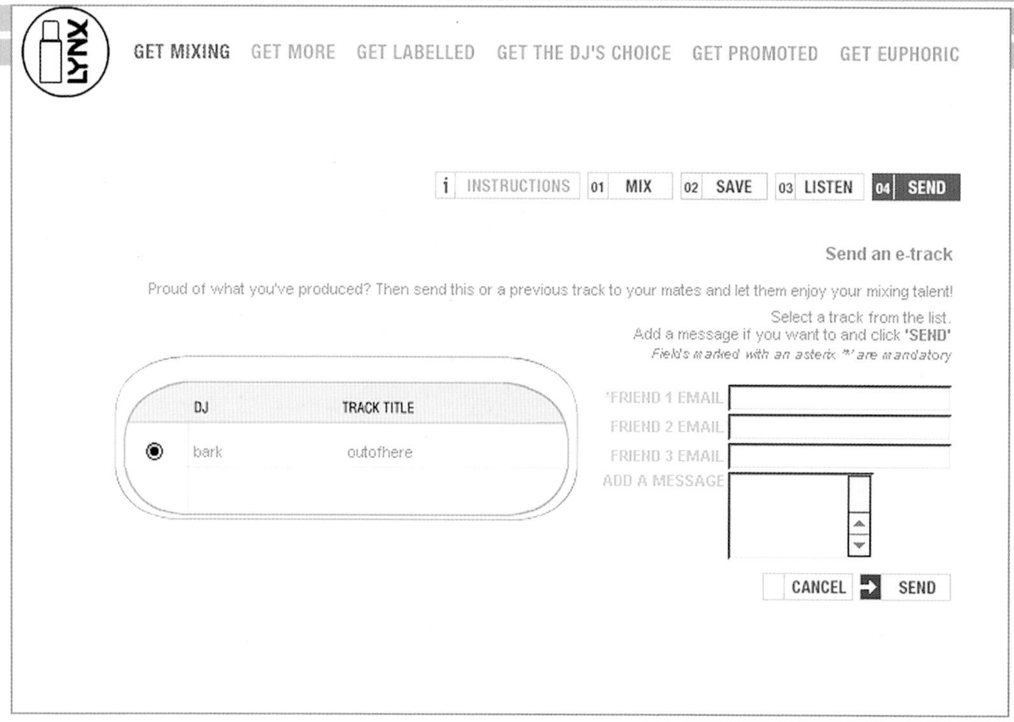

LYNX GET MIXING   GET MORE   GET LABELLED   GET THE DJ'S CHOICE   GET PROMOTED   GET EUPHORIC

ℹ INSTRUCTIONS 01 MIX 02 SAVE 03 LISTEN 04 **SEND**

Send an e-track

Proud of what you've produced? Then send this or a previous track to your mates and let them enjoy your mixing talent!

Select a track from the list.
Add a message if you want to and click **'SEND'**
Fields marked with an asterix '*' are mandatory

DJ	TRACK TITLE
⊙ bark	outofhere

*FRIEND 1 EMAIL [   ]
FRIEND 2 EMAIL [   ]
FRIEND 3 EMAIL [   ]
ADD A MESSAGE [   ]

CANCEL ➔ SEND

Send

Send

Send

PLAYLIFE
WWW.PLAYLIFE.COM S/S 2002

CLOSE WINDOWS

Fill out the form and then click the preview button

Send to (name)   e-mail address

From (name)   Your e-mail address

Message (only 250 characters will be accepted):

N° characters

 Send   Clear

Send

Send

Send

Send

> COMPANY   > POSTCARDS
> PRODUCTS   DESKTOP
> STORES   SCREENSAVER
> EVENTS   SLIDESHOW
> FREE PLAY
> SITEMAP

POSTCARDS
Select the one you like and send it.

> [playlife.net] Playlife is a Benetton sports brand and offers users postcards which they can send to friends by email with their own personal messages.

CREATING INTEREST **SEARCH ENGINE OPTIMIZATION**

[webgravity.co.uk] Webgravity is one of a number of companies which can advise sites on how to ensure they get the best rankings in search engines and directories.

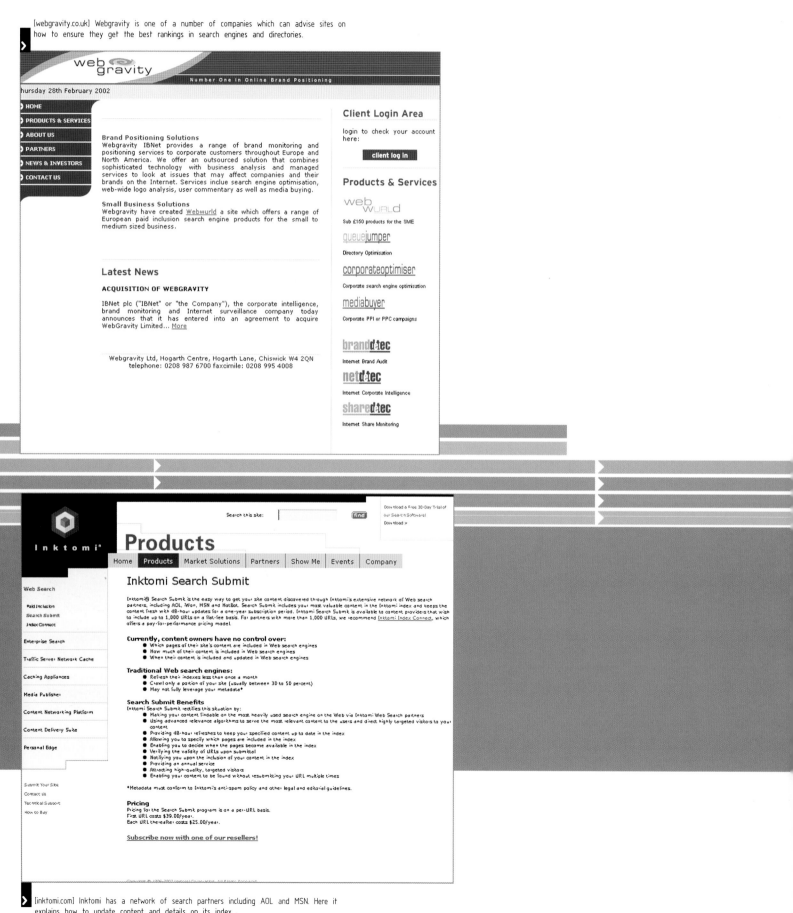

[inktomi.com] Inktomi has a network of search partners including AOL and MSN. Here it explains how to update content and details on its index.

One of the biggest sources of new traffic online is search engines. By definition, users turn to such mechanisms or sites to find a site related to a particular query. Google, which is famed for its simple interface, now offers direct access to three billion web documents, it claims. It responds to more than 150 million queries a day.

Whereas a few years ago, the use of search engines was quite straightforward, more recently the waters have become slightly muddied as sites like AltaVista tried to grow beyond their search engine origins and effectively turn into mainstream portals. AltaVista has since declared its intention to return to its roots and now offers a more streamlined and straightforward interface to highlight its search function. There has also been the rise of the paid-for search engines like the US-based Overture, which used to be called GoTo, and European player Espotting. The way these search engines make money is that advertisers pay to be listed high up in search results. Basically, advertisers bid on words and phrases – keywords – relevant to their web site. The higher the bid, the higher the site appears in the listings. A further development is the number of non-search engine sites offering search facilities from their own pages using technology provided by the major search engines.

A new breed of businesses, called Search Engine Optimization companies, has emerged, offering services to get sites higher up on search listings. Most such companies are brought in at the end of the development process to help sites improve their showing in automatically compiled listings. For instance, search engines look at the frequency of certain search keywords on a web page. More frequent use of a word increases the site's overall relevancy.

Hallam Smallpiece, technical account manager of Search Engine Optimization company Webgravity, says that designers can help the process by taking heed of such considerations early on in the development of a site. One key factor is that '99 per cent' of search engines are not up to speed with the latest developments in technology. 'Google has only just started to read Pdf files,' he says. 'Many web sites are not being made with search engines in mind.' Sites that face problems with search engines are those which depend on dynamic content. 'It is sites which are hideously dynamic like the booking service for an airline or something that is driven by a gambling mechanism that need to be aware of this,' Smallpiece warns. 'It is dynamic and database driven sites which are bad in this respect.' Html text-based sites should have less of a problem.

One way of maximising the chance of being picked by a search engine is to have more than one point or page of entry to a site, suggests Smallpiece: 'If you have fifteen possible introduction pages, you become more pertinent to more searches than if you only have one.' Ultimately, though, it is a site's content that is searched, which means that the more relevant it is, the better the chance of being picked up by the search engines. 'If you duplicate the points of entry, and therefore the relevant keywords, it helps,' says Smallpiece, 'but having good, relevant content which does get updated is the key.'

[altavista.com] Major search engines like AltaVista tell site owners how to submit their web site address for ranking in relevant searches.

CREATING INTEREST **LINKS & DEALS**

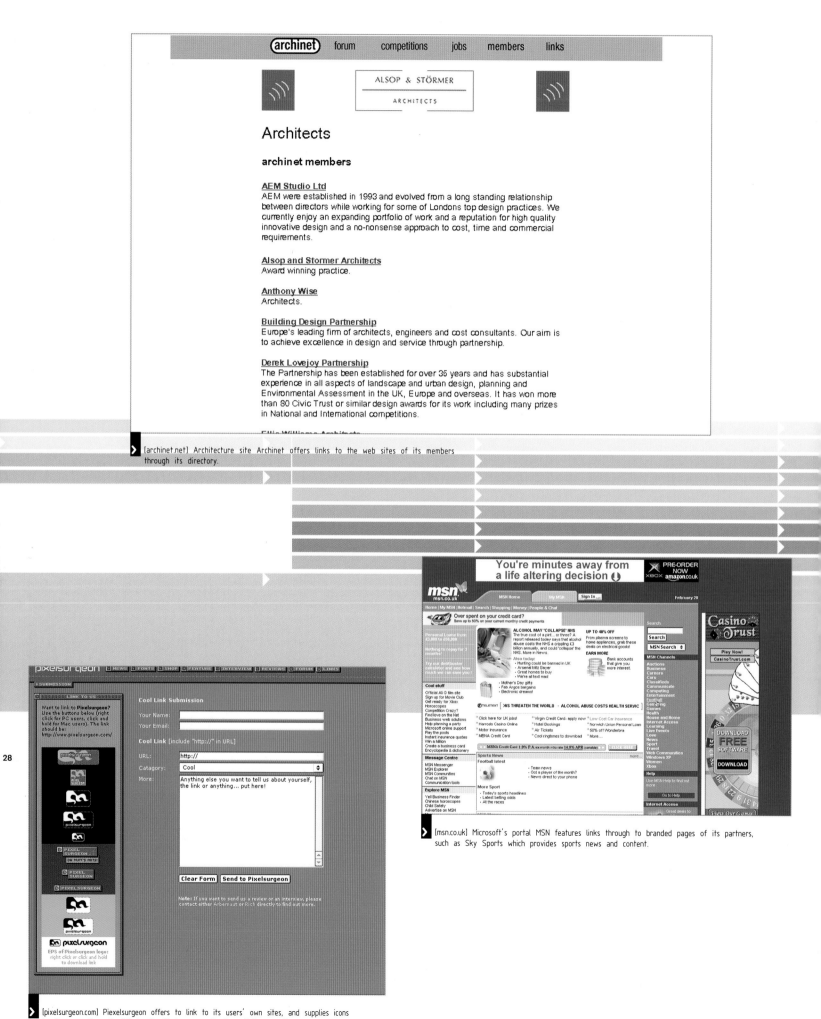

[archinet.net] Architecture site Archinet offers links to the web sites of its members through its directory.

[msn.co.uk] Microsoft's portal MSN features links through to branded pages of its partners, such as Sky Sports which provides sports news and content.

[pixelsurgeon.com] Piexelsurgeon offers to link to its users' own sites, and supplies icons to those wanting to link to the Pixelsurgeon site from their own sites.

An obvious source of traffic for any web site is the users of other web sites. Not only are these people already online, but it is easier to get someone to click from one site to another than to entice a shopper to walk out of one store and into another.

One source of traffic is from portal sites – which as the name suggests, act as gateways to the web, and direct large volumes of traffic to other sites. These can either be the major, international portals such as Yahoo!, MSN, AOL Time Warner, Microsoft and the Lycos Network (identified in October 2001 by Nielsen//NetRatings as the top five global web properties as used by people with Internet access at home) or smaller specialist portal sites that act as a comprehensive resource or web directory for one subject area. However, for providing a share of their traffic, the portals will often want something in return. This can take the form of a basic boost to the bottom line – where a site will pay directly to be listed by the portal, or enter into some other form of commercial agreement (if an etailer is added to a portal site taking the form of a shopping mall, for example, a revenue share agreement might be struck). But other arrangements can also be made, such as the provision of content to the portal site in exchange for listing. Some portals will list sites for free in order to be the definitive resource in their subject area on the web.

Alternatives exist in the form of reciprocal link-swaps, where two sites, each of whose users may be interested in the other site, agree to link to one another. This can be valuable even when the two sites are 'competitors' as it demonstrates openness and confidence on the part of the site owners. A logical expansion of this idea is seen with the growth of web rings – which are effectively communities of sites on a similar theme. A web ring aggregates users of sites which have a relatively small audience and builds them into an easy-to-find community. Each site in the ring should link to two others – one before and one after. If a user clicked the 'next' link on each site, they should eventually end up where they started.

Portals like Yahoo! are ideally placed to host such rings of sites. Yahoo! WebRings showcases a range of sites dealing with topics ranging from business and finance to sex and romance. Yahoo! itself, now one of the major online businesses and brands, grew up from humble origins as a directory of links set up by two Stanford University students.

[skysports.com] Broadcaster Sky Sports offers content on its own site but also allows its content to feature in partnerships with sites like the portal MSN.

[totopools.com] Going through links on the msn.co.uk homepage to Sky Sports and from there to Toto Pools, the betting site, produces a page designed with all three brands featured.

29

CREATING INTEREST **PROMOTIONS**

Internet research company Forrester, predicts that web-based promotions could be worth up to $14 billion a year by 2006. According to a spokesperson from US-based agency Promotions.com, this is because of the results offered by web-based promotions, which range from offering money-off incentives to providing prizes for games and contests. Amie Smith says consumer response rates can be up to five times higher for web promotions than for non-web-based promotions. Primarily the aim is to promote sales of a product, predominantly offline, but this can serve to drive users to a web site as well.

Promotions can take many shapes or forms, and are often limited only by the willingness of a brand or company involved to link up online and offline activities. For instance, the soft drink Lucozade tied up with the debut of the Tomb Raider film in cinemas and effectively rebranded itself on bottles as Larazade. A special competition site was built at Larazade.com to tie in with a promotion on the bottle's packaging. Lucozade offered users the chance to win adventure weekends away after completing a game on the web site based around the drink giving the heroine Lara Croft enough energy to complete a set of tasks.

Beer brand Boddingtons has a featured competition page at its site boddingtons.com. Like most promotions, the key is to get as many people as possible to enter and therefore provide the site with details for potential marketing and research purposes. Hence the questions posed are not meant to be difficult – in fact, the Boddingtons site even provides a text link to the part of the site where the answer can be found.

▶ [colgate2in1.com] Toothpaste brand Colgate 2in1 offers visitors to its web site the chance to win a luxury holiday.

‹ BACK   › FORWARD

HOME | MINI INTERNATIONAL | WAYS TO PAY | OUR VALUES | CONTACT & FAQs

OUR CARS   BUILD YOUR OWN   FIND A DEALER   GET IN THE LOOP   GEAR UP   **MOTOR ON**

DESKTOP IMAGES

It's our daily routine: disciplined relaxation, focused wandering, and meditating upon desktop images of the MINI Cooper and MINI Cooper S.

› [www.miniusa.com] The US site for the Mini promotes the car by offering users the chance to go 'desktop motoring' with screensavers and images for their PCs.

[threadless.com] T-shirt retailer Threadless.com asks users to submit designs, which are voted on by visitors to the site. Winners have their designs made up into T-shirts which are then sold by the site.

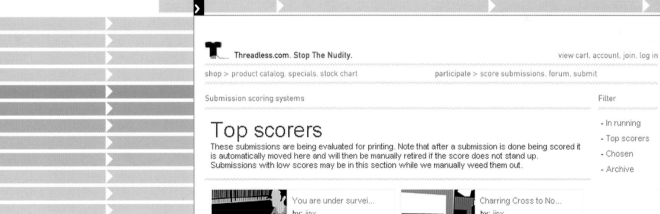

T **Threadless.com. Stop The Nudity.**   view cart, account, join, log in

shop > product catalog, specials, stock chart   participate > score submissions, forum, submit

Submission scoring systems   Filter

Top scorers

These submissions are being evaluated for printing. Note that after a submission is done being scored it is automatically moved here and will then be manually retired if the score does not stand up. Submissions with low scores may be in this section while we manually weed them out.

- In running
- Top scorers
- Chosen
- Archive

You are under survei...
by: jinx
ttl score: 638, 209 ppl

Charring Cross to No...
by: jinx
ttl score: 689, 218 ppl

use{love}abuse™
by: iFDL
ttl score: 643, 260 ppl

left right left
by: eddyizm
ttl score: 605, 262 ppl

The 8 steps to my he...
by: Ugly
ttl score: 679, 259 ppl

GRRR
by: jinx
ttl score: 608, 239 ppl

choice
by: cybra
ttl score: 983, 312 ppl

Angelina Jolie
by: noxious
ttl score: 788, 315 ppl

loveliest of seasons
by: beecee

beetles for everyone...
by: drewheffron

> COMPANY
> PRODUCTS
> STORES
> EVENTS
> FREE PLAY
> SITEMAP

Playlife
The youngest brand of the Benetton' sports world is a clothing and footwear collection designed for maximum comfort in leisure and sports.

PLAYLIFE PRESENTS: 105 ALTA QUOTA

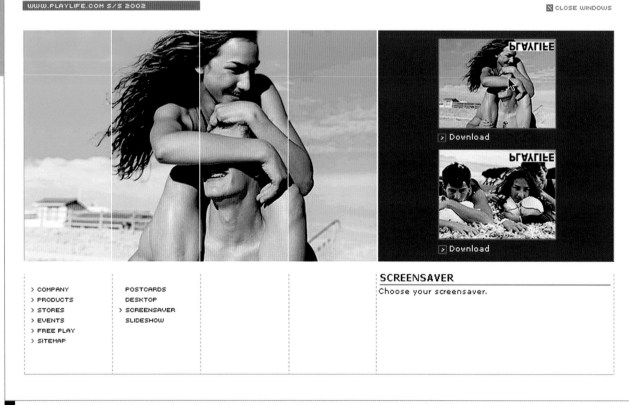

> Download

> Download

> COMPANY   POSTCARDS
> PRODUCTS   DESKTOP
> STORES   > SCREENSAVER
> EVENTS   SLIDESHOW
> FREE PLAY
> SITEMAP

SCREENSAVER
Choose your screensaver.

[playlife.net] Benetton's sportswear brand promotes itself by giving away digital freebies from screen savers to wallpaper for PCs

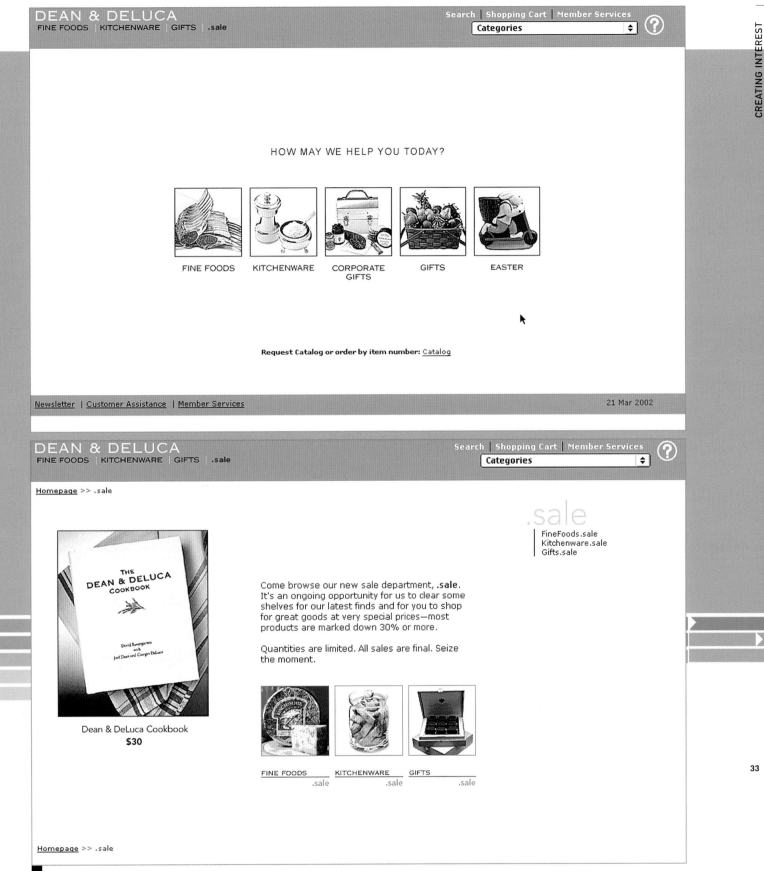

DEAN & DELUCA
FINE FOODS | KITCHENWARE | GIFTS | .sale

Search | Shopping Cart | Member Services ⑦
Categories ▲▼

HOW MAY WE HELP YOU TODAY?

FINE FOODS   KITCHENWARE   CORPORATE GIFTS   GIFTS   EASTER

Request Catalog or order by item number: Catalog

Newsletter | Customer Assistance | Member Services   21 Mar 2002

DEAN & DELUCA
FINE FOODS | KITCHENWARE | GIFTS | .sale

Search | Shopping Cart | Member Services ⑦
Categories ▲▼

Homepage >> .sale

.sale
FineFoods.sale
Kitchenware.sale
Gifts.sale

Dean & DeLuca Cookbook
$30

Come browse our new sale department, **.sale**.
It's an ongoing opportunity for us to clear some
shelves for our latest finds and for you to shop
for great goods at very special prices—most
products are marked down 30% or more.

Quantities are limited. All sales are final. Seize
the moment.

FINE FOODS   KITCHENWARE   GIFTS
              .sale   .sale   .sale

Homepage >> .sale

[deanddeluca.com] Retailer Dean & Deluca has a dedicated area on its site for its own sale stock.

CREATING INTEREST OFFLINE ADVERTISING

At the height of the boom in the number of new dotcom start-ups in the US and Europe in March 2000, offline advertising seemed to be the only accepted way to build an online brand and often, it appeared, formed the basis of the business plan.

Not only have lessons been learnt since then, but the offline audience should also have become more web-savvy and able to distinguish the different messages from dotcoms as opposed to asking itself the question, after a 30-second TV slot from AOL, 'What's an ISP?' It is difficult enough to explain to an unfamiliar audience what an ISP is, let alone why your service is better than that of a rival, particularly in less than a minute.

However, Internet Service Providers and financial sites have filled the top slots of online spenders offline, says Guy Abrahams, strategy director of media-buying specialist Carat. According to figures compiled by ACNielsen MMS for Carat, UK dotcoms spent some £24 million on offline advertising – print, cinema, radio, outdoor and television executions – in October 2001.

Some forms of offline advertising have been particularly effective. Priceline, the discount 'name your own price' travel e-tailer, has used celebrity radio slots to promote its web site. It makes sense to think that people might listen to the radio while surfing the web – even while at work. It is less likely that they are online and watching TV at the same time.

Established and traditional businesses have got used to promoting their web sites via their offline advertising, and in the case of retailers, their high street outlets and shops. One British retailer, the frozen foods giant Iceland, rebranded as www.iceland.co.uk to get the message to its customers. Many smaller-scale businesses have taken similar steps, replacing their names with their web addesses on everything from the shop front to giveaway pens and keyrings.

And nothing is quite so effective as a fully integrated marketing campaign, which combines on- and offline elements. This thought gives rise to the pan-European plans of Finnish telecoms company Nokia to promote itself. Its Nokia game allows players to be contacted through a variety of channels – from SMS (text messaging) to email – as they seek to solve the puzzle.

Offline marketing can get people to go online but the fact is that it needs to be especially creative to explain the benefits of a digital channel to an offline audience. After all, if that was an easy process, the interactivity offered by digital channels – from interactive television to the world-wide web itself – would not be such an appealing prospect for advertisers.

[Lastminute.com] The travel etailer lastminute.com can attribute much of its brand recognition to extensive advertising undertaken throughout the site's history. Unusual media, ranging from sandwich bags and the exit doors of Heathrow airport, were used in addition to newspaper and poster advertising.

> [stepstone.com advertising] StepStone used a high profile television advertising campaign in the UK to link its online recruitment business with major sports and sporting events.

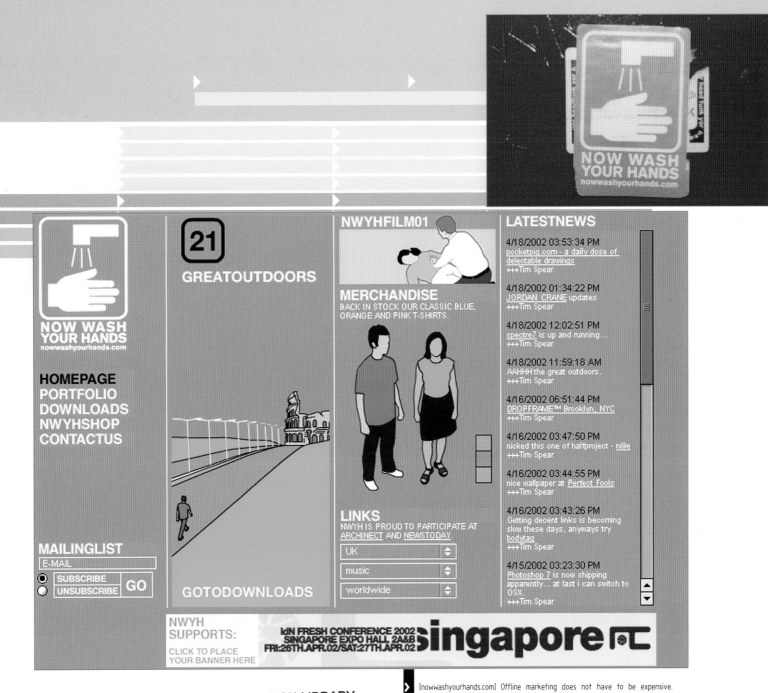

> [nowwashyourhands.com] Offline marketing does not have to be expensive. Nowwashyourhands.com was emblazoned on stickers which could be seen on the back door of toilet cubicles in public places such as pubs.

CREATING INTEREST **EVENTS**

Scheduled events, either taking place online, or happening offline and broadcast on the web, can be a useful way of attracting large numbers of users to a site.

In December 2000, Microsoft's MSN portal sponsored a one-off concert by Madonna, her first UK appearance in concert for several years, and offered an exclusive webcast to those fans without tickets. The actual number of people who viewed the web cast online has been debated – MSN claimed officially that it received nine million hits on the night in question – but one thing seems certain, MSN's sponsorship and webcasting of Madonna's one-off gig gained it plenty in terms of marketing and PR value for the site. MSN repeated the trick by exclusively showing an Italian Elton John concert in July 2001.

Likewise, the European Internet Service Provider Tiscali, linked up with Irish rock band U2 and its web site at www.u2.com in a deal to broadcast a US concert to European users in October 2001.

Smaller sites, such as that of the chef Delia Smith, also use live scheduled interviews or audience question and answer sessions to increase traffic.

In a twist on the idea of the offline event broadcast online, the UK snack food brand Ginsters has launched its own permanent rock event to bring its brand to a new audience. Ginsters, which is better known for sausage rolls than rock and roll, has pushed its virtual and animated rock concert site Pastonbury, featuring music from real if little known bands, as a festival without the mud.

Pastonbury, of course, is not truly live, but benefits from the impression that it is. Likewise, updating the content of a site at a specific predetermined time can have a similar impact, as although users may not log on at exactly that time, they may make a mental note to visit soon after.

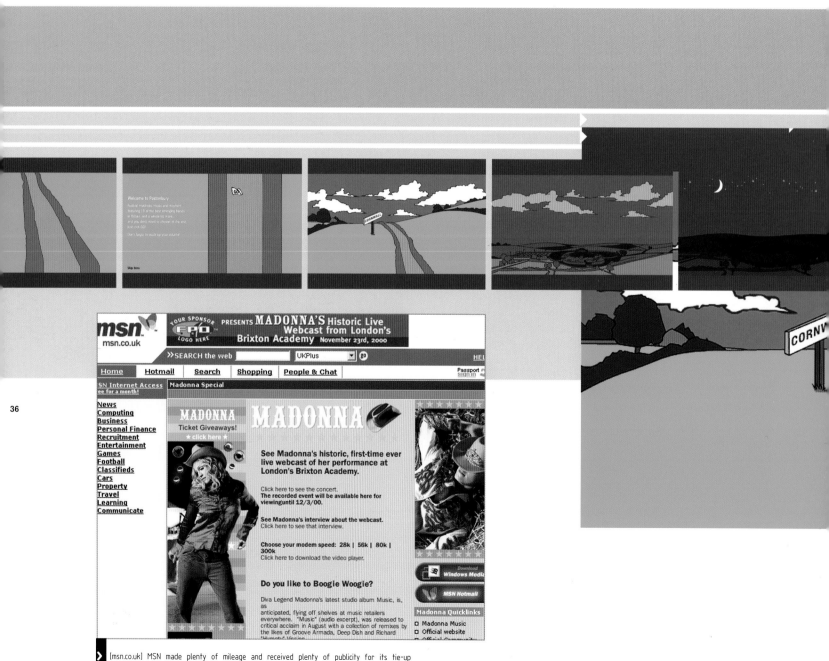

[msn.co.uk] MSN made plenty of mileage and received plenty of publicity for its tie-up with Madonna to webcast a concert she was playing in London.

14 September 2001

mozz : How does it feel to have finished the book? Can't wait to see it!!

Delia Smith: Hello Mozz. In one way it feels like being let out of prison. But in another way, it's very scary because I'm always afraid there will be a mistake. So can you say a little prayer that there isn't?!

jean : Is Kikkoman Soy Sauce safe to use?

Delia Smith: Hi Jean. Kikkoman Soy Sauce is made from soy beans, salt, water and wheat. It's the best one I've used and doesn't contain any additives. I have been to Japan and seen the whole process. It is one of the purest condiments in the world.

jamie : Hi Delia, What do you think about Jamie Oliver becoming a dad?

Delia Smith: Hi Jamie. I think it's wonderful news and I'm sure he'll be a very good dad.

ann y : Friends of ours have recently moved house & have two apple trees in their new garden. Do you have any recipes for using up large amounts of apples, apart from apple sauce & apple pie? Also can they store their surplus? And if so, how? Thanks.

Delia Smith: Hello Ann Y. We have tonnes of apple recipes on the site. For lots of apples I would recommend making chutney, and most of my recipes have large amounts of apples in them. If you want to store apples, you can only do this if they are perfect and not bruised. But if you wrap each apple in a piece of newspaper and store them in cardboard boxes in a cool place, or if you have a cold loft with no heating, you can store them on a shelf side by side. Don't forget you can always use them for

[deliaonline.com] Even smaller scale sites can use scheduled events and chats or question and answer exchanges with experts and well-known figures to get users to visit the site at a particular time.

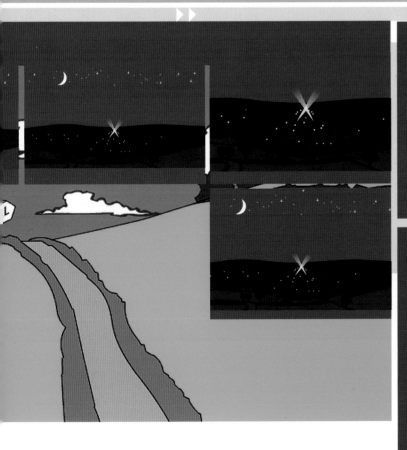

37

[pastonbury.co.uk] The Pastonbury web site, which belongs to snack brand Ginsters, deliberately tries to capture all the trappings of a rock festival online from building a sense of anticipation as users go through the site to the gig, and hearing music from 'live' bands.

01

CREATING INTEREST **SPONSORSHIP & PR**

Online sponsorship is an increasingly common way for brands and web-based businesses to attract the attention of new audiences, and build brand values through association with whatever is being sponsored.

Sponsorship does not in itself produce large volumes of traffic for the sponsor, however, as a key difference between online advertising and sponsorship is that the aim of sponsorship is to keep the user on the site they originally visited. The aim of advertising, on the other hand, is usually to drive the user through to the advertiser's site directly.

Sponsorship works more effectively for the sponsor when its site or product is relevant to what is being sponsored, or when it can provide relevant content to the host site. For example, Sol, linked up with the clubbing web site ministryofsound.com. The Mexican beer brand chose to attract attention with an animated game, which asked users to pilot a plane, avoiding barriers and parachuting crates of beer on to certain targets. Success was rewarded by offers of cases of beer.

Public relations (PR) is another way of building a web site's profile and raising awareness among new audiences. PR is a discipline of marketing which is all about building the image of an organisation in the public's eyes through media channels. A significant advantage of PR over some other forms of communications activity is that the result is an article in a magazine or newspaper, or an item on a TV show, which is judged to be more authoritative

and true than advertising by readers and viewers. PR can also be very precisely targetted towards the sort of niche media – such as trade magazines – that a specific target audience is likely to read. The scattergun approach, of sending the same press release to every news organisation, is a waste of time and money.

If a site has a story to tell about its aims and achievements, PR can be a relatively cost effective way of getting its name and URL known to a wider audience. At its most basic, PR should centre around significant business developments – from news of a new investor to a significant landmark – say getting a certain number of page impressions a week – in the site's growth. Of course, this information can be of interest to the site's users as well as journalists and media outlets.

More obviously the benefits of PR can be seen in terms of building traffic to a web site. When a story is picked up by Internet media-owners and online offshoots of media outlets, they not only publish the piece, and put links to their own archive so that users can drill down and get more depth and information on a story without being overloaded, but they also link to the site itself, providing immediate access for the curious.

Many web sites recognise the value of media coverage and contain a press area on the site that contains press releases and media contact information, and possibly photographs or screen shots.

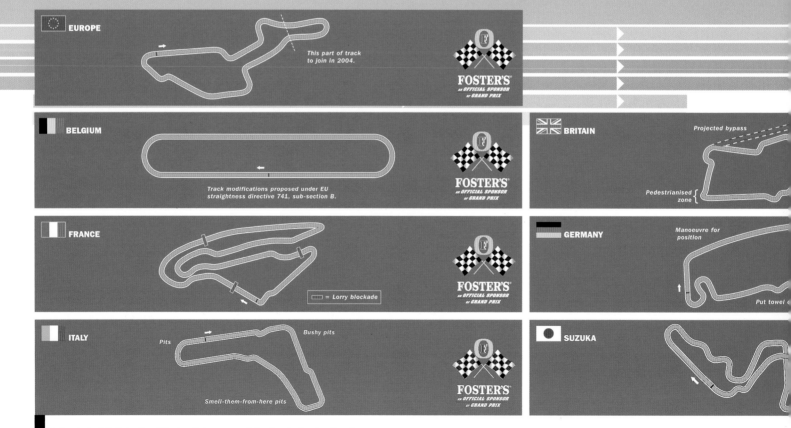

[fosters badges] Foster's, the drinks brand, has sponsored the Formula 1 racing site of the British television network ITV.

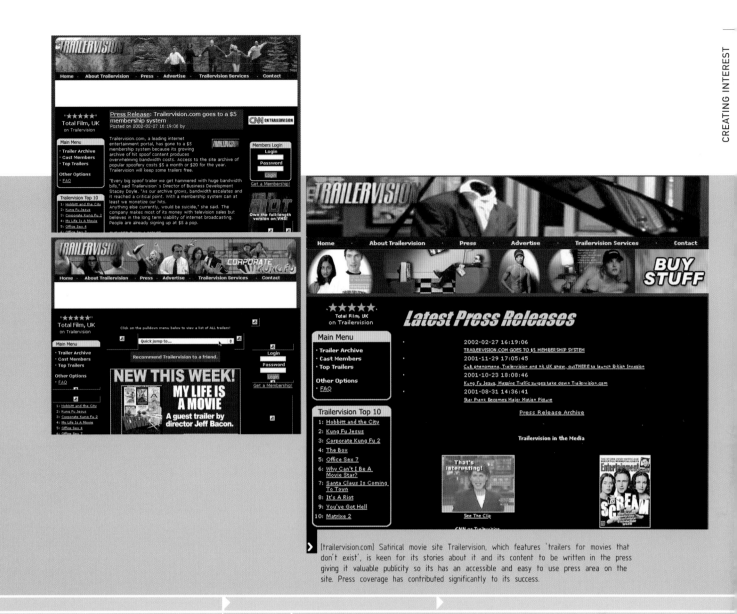

[trailervision.com] Satirical movie site Trailervision, which features 'trailers for movies that don't exist', is keen for its stories about it and its content to be written in the press giving it valuable publicity so its has an accessible and easy to use press area on the site. Press coverage has contributed significantly to its success.

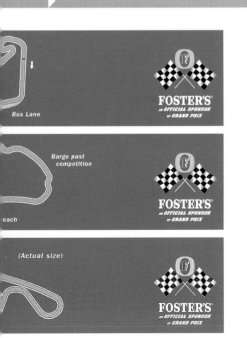

[crocus.co.uk] The gardening web site Crocus has benefitted from extensive press coverage. Its press section aids journalists wanting to write about the site by providing downloadable logos and high resolution photographs, as well as press releases.

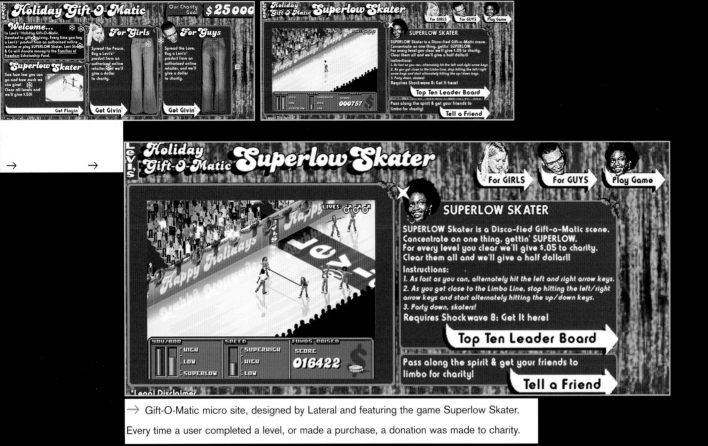

→ Gift-O-Matic micro site, designed by Lateral and featuring the game Superlow Skater. Every time a user completed a level, or made a purchase, a donation was made to charity.

WHAT'S THIS SITE ALL ABOUT?

WHAT'S THIS SITE ALL ABOUT?

MOVIE

SKIP INTRO >>

IN THIS CASE WE ARE FOLLOWING THREE NEW TARGETS

BOYD, JEFF, SARAH.

WANTED
For Wearing a name Tag.

WANTED
On spurious charges.

SKIP INTRO >>

WHAT'S IN IT FOR YOU?

AND YOU'LL HAVE THE OPPORTUNITY TO JOIN US AND WIN A BUNCH OF COOL GEAR IN THE PROCESS.

SKIP INTRO >>

→ Lost Change – a surveillance-themed micro site linked to twelve 'lost' micro sites, which create a single journey through games, music, competitions and video footage.

→   Levi's

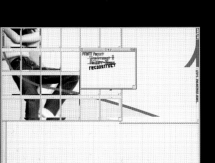

Left: experimental pop-up-based micro site, by Lateral
Below: LostAirport.com micro site, by Lateral

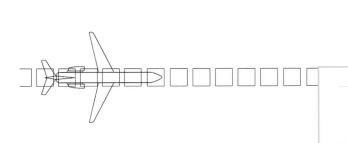

lostairport

Enter the Lost
POD universe

Click to download
Quicktime

This site is best viewed with Internet Explorer 4+ and Netscape 4.5+ b...

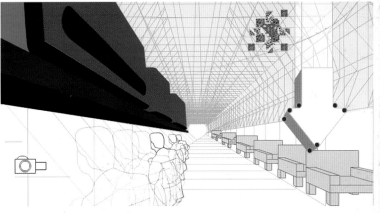

Although the familiar shape of the banner advert is still the staple tool of online advertisers, the work of companies like Unicast in the US, which developed rich media Superstitial ads, and Tangozebra in the UK, have introduced new formats to engage users and induce them to click through to the advertisers' web sites.

Yet, it is still the advertisers which are responsible for the executions and ultimately take the risk with their brand and campaigns to trial new formats online. Jeans brand Levi Strauss was one of the first mainstream advertisers to get acclaim for its innovative use of new ad formats. It has been advertising online since 1995, according to Jon Bains, chairman of UK digital agency Lateral which, in the USA, is the digital agency of record for Levi's.

In 1999 the company debuted its use of overts to much acclaim. The ads coincided with the rise of the brand's Flat Eric icon, and saw an animation of the fluffy yellow figure effectively parachute down the screen. Clicking on the figure sent the user to Levis.com. In Spring 2000 it tried out an innovative use of real estate on a web site by sponsoring the actual '404 Error Page' on Yahoo! UK and Ireland for a time when promoting the Twisted Original jean in Spring 2000. Users who typed in the wrong web address when going through the portal were greeted with a Levi's branded page, created by Lateral, rather than just another standard error page. Users got a series of messages which were designed to 'enliven' the frustrating experience of getting something wrong. Cue more awareness of the brand. The Error Pages campaign delivered some 4.8 million impressions across Europe, according to Lateral.

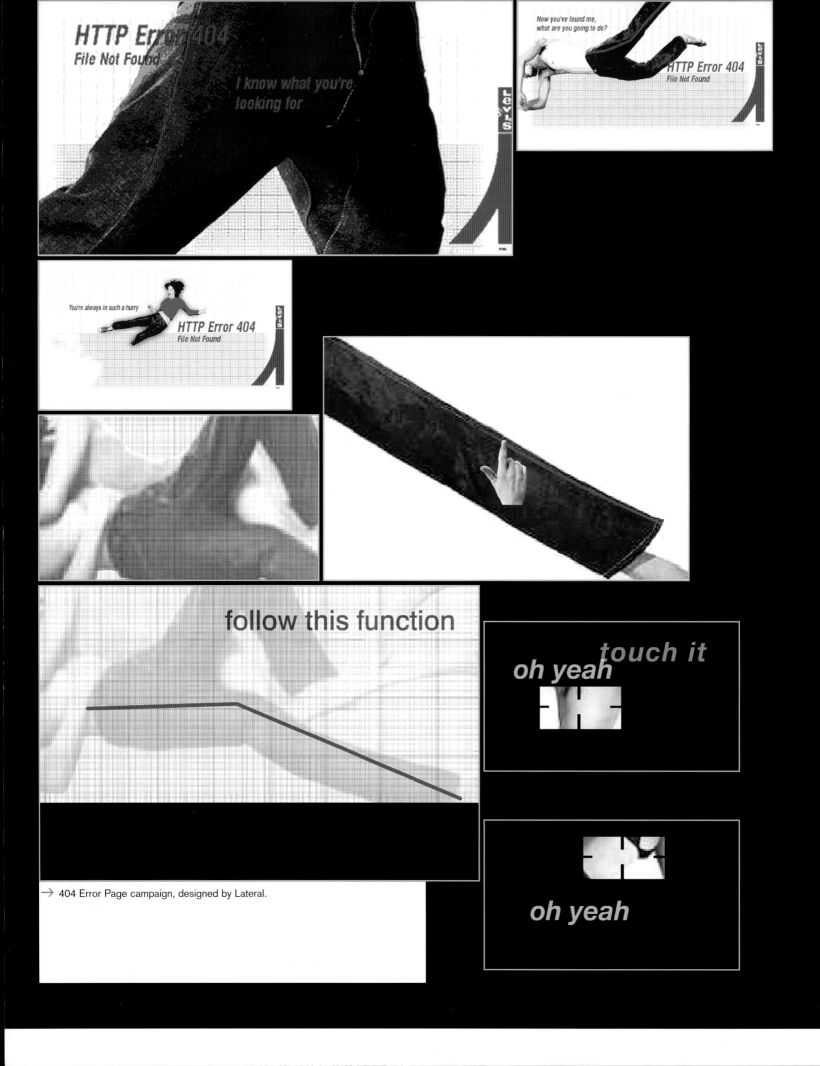

→ 404 Error Page campaign, designed by Lateral.

→ Lost Arcade games micro site, designed by Lateral.

Initially, Levi's used traditional brand equity scores to measure success, though in the US at least, it is also concerned that advertising should drive traffic to its range of sites, which include a wide variety of micro sites, which often sit on the main Levis.com web site. Bains explains: 'In general, you build a micro-site when you don't want to mess around with the core content of the main site.'

This means that Levi's can maintain a presence on its core web site and introduce micro-sites for each new campaign or product launch. A micro site designed for the Twisted range of Engineered jeans is one such example. It tapped into the power of viral marketing to get users to the bespoke site, which encouraged users to send digicards to their friends, enabling Levi's to gather two email addresses for the price of one registration. Web agency Good Technology and advertising agency Bartle Bogle Hegarty developed a site which users accessed once they had got sent an email asking them to play with Twisted Boy who is hidden away in the offline television ad campaign. The site is also accessible through the main Levi's site where users are encouraged to play a game by altering the animated figure's limbs. It doesn't end there as they are sent even more limbs by email.

The numerous elements of Levi's online presence in recent years have encompassed games and music, reportage and filmed documentary footage, an eclectic mix unified by a quirky sensibility. Whatever the execution, the voice is identifiably Levi's. Ultimately, when working with the company, says Bains, the brand is key. 'A brand is a brand and it has its own tone and language. In the case of Levi's, the brand rules are more important than the rules that you may have in mind to build a site.'

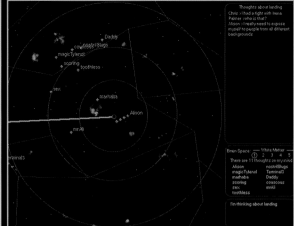

→ Above and right: Pages from the twelve 'lost' microsites, including lostshock, lostmarrakech, lostequipment and lostfetish, all by Lateral.

Below: Animated micro site for Levi's Engineered jeans, by Bartle Bogle Hegarty and Good Technology.

02

MAINTAINING INTEREST

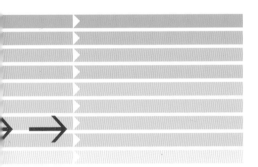

MAINTAINING INTEREST **INTRODUCTION**

The sheer numbers of people coming online and using the Internet day-by-day mean that piquing their interest, intriguing them, and getting them to actually visit a web site is not as difficult as it could be. The trick is getting them to spend time on the site and not only enabling them to do what they want to do, but helping them help the site fulfil its function.

Again, this depends on the nature of the site, but the big question is what the user wants from the online experience itself. This highlights the effective use of the right channels to get the right users to come to a site.

Users expecting a literary discussion forum may be upset, as well as effectively useless to the site, if they have been erroneously directed to an online bookstore. Not only are they useless now, but they could also be reluctant to return when they do indeed want to buy a book in the future. Again, traffic can be useful but only if it is the right traffic.

However, an even bigger problem potentially is that the user does not get the right message about the site as soon as they arrive – what is the site; what's on it; why should you, the user, stick around to find out? It is one thing to find that you are on the wrong site; it is another to find that out after aimlessly trying to navigate through a variety of options and pathways, waiting for a big image to download, or watching an animated prelude to the main event – ultimately, wasting valuable time. Many users, used to disappointment and frustration, now give sites very little time to demonstrate that they have what the user wants.

Key to this is the site's brand. Hopefully, this will have been built up by the effort to bring people to the site and once they arrive they should be sure of what they are getting. But if brands are a 'promise', what users get when they arrive at the site must be the fulfilment of that promise. First, the user must recognise through visual clues that this is the site they were looking for. European sports content site Sports.com has made sure that this is fairly and squarely the case. Colour coding is an important factor here and its name is at the centre and top of its homepage. In the US, there has been a move towards 'better and more consistent online branding,' notes Dagny Pieto, art director at web agency Bluewave USA. She explains that this is particularly notable in the big corporations: 'Up until very recently, a lot of big corporations didn't really understand the importance of giving customers a single consistent face for all their communications online in the way that they do offline.'

▶ [cowfighter.com] Even when the Flash-based games site, Cowfighter.com, is loading, designers Global Beach keep users occupied with a lively animated intro to the 'fight'.

Imagination Group Profile Resources The Imagination Group Profile Resources News The Imagination Group Profile Resources News e Imaginat
People Work People Work Contact People Work Contact

Predators - eat or be eaten?

redators - eat or be
aten?

ew book about
magination published
y Phaidon

magination helps
ricsson bring Mobile
nternet to life

atest news

A new family exhibition opens at The Natural History Museum on July 18th 2001. Designed by Imagination, Predators will allow visitors to see first hand the skill and cunning that decides whether an animal gets a meal, or becomes one.

Open to Visitors from 18th July 2001 - 6th May 2002

Working with The Natural History Museum's in-house researchers, Imagination's multidisciplinary team developed the overall creative strategy; including the exhibition theme, storyline, environment, graphics, identity and lighting.

Imagination has provided concepts for an integrated marketing campaign for the exhibition. The development of the graphic identity guidelines has helped inform marketing collateral such as promotional materials and merchandise.

Imagination architect Paulo Pimentel said: "Predators is visually stunning. Rather than trying to capture realistic environments we have used abstract imagery to create a sinister world where visitors learn what 'survival of the fittest' really means."

Predators is an exploration of attack and defence in the natural world. Visitors can:

· Try on the ear of a bat-eared fox and discover how a keen sense of hearing can improve your chance of searching out prey

[imagination.com] Design company Imagination's site includes content such as a news section and updates on its projects to give visitors extra reasons to return. Its horizontal scroll bar is another feature which is there to make the curious linger on the site and get it to stand out from the crowd.

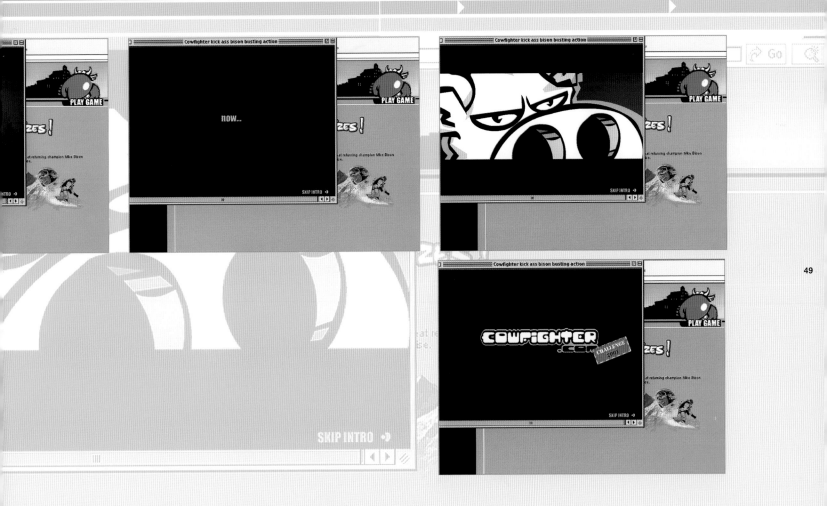

MAINTAINING INTEREST **INTRODUCTION**

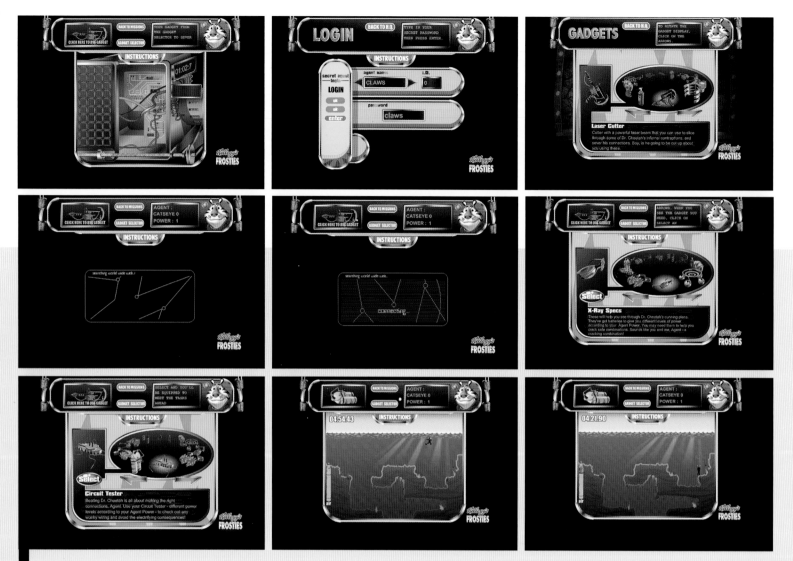

▷ [frosties.co.uk] The web site of Kellogg's breakfast cereal Frosties encourages young users to interact with its representative, Tony the Tiger, through games.

The same principle – that increasingly sophisticated users are less likely to give sites the benefit of the doubt – should inform all other aspects of the design. Navigating around the site should be easy and intuitive – a user should not have to work too hard to find the content that they want and, if the branding is correct, expect. Unusual mapping or navigational systems on web sites sound distinctive and visually interesting in theory, but in practice need to be applied very carefully to avoid losing users at a fast rate. Exceptions can of course be made where the audience is likely to positively relish the adventure of an experimental navigation system, but these instances are few and far between.

As technologies developed that allowed site designers to add animation, sound, film and other forms of bandwidth sapping content to web sites, it was assumed that users would appreciate these things. At the time, this may even have been true – there was a level of excitement about a revolutionary medium in its infancy that made us tolerant of long waits, broken connections and charming, but essentially pointless distractions from the main function of the site. There is still a role to play for animation, film, sound and the rest – the web is a dynamic, interactive, hybrid medium – but designers should always be aware that as the web has now become part of the furniture of our lives, we expect it, perhaps unreasonably, to cause as little or less trouble than extracting information from a magazine or buying something from a convenience store.

Design has a role to play in making content accessible and interesting to look at, or transactions clear and navigable, but it should never get in the way of the content or hold up the transaction. For instance, Macromedia Flash, the software tool which allows animations on the web page, is often derided as off-putting for users. It does have its fans as well and is appropriate on a site aimed at an audience familiar with it – but sites built entirely in Flash not only exclude potential users accessing the web from a computer that is not Flash-enabled, but are also off-putting to those who just want to locate information quickly.

Usability, as championed by web design gurus like Jakob Nielsen, is key to ensuring that the core messages of a site are heard. Ultimately, it is about putting the user at the centre of the web experience and ensuring that the needs and wants of the user are kept at the heart of the development process.

[ribena.co.uk] As with many food and drink brands, fruit drink Ribena has a site that features games and other entertainment services to encourage users – particularly children in this case – to interact with the brand and its animated representatives online.

51

MAINTAINING INTEREST **TECHNOLOGY**

For many the golden rule is that slow download times are a serious problem. Specialist software requirements – such as Flash, Shockwave or Real Audio Player – aside, if the user's modem is slow (and their connection is usually slower than that of the web designer), they could be left with a negative impression of the site and a frustrating experience.

Sites should be designed to take account of the differing technologies that users are likely to have. While some users will be able to experience Flash content, others will not and will want to be able to view the same content as static text and images. Similarly, sites should be tested for compatibility with both PC and Macintosh machines, and the leading browser types, from

▶ [chlorophyll.co.in] Indian web developer and brand consultancy chlorophyll uses Flash-based animation to give its web site a hi-tech 3-D effect and conjure images of science fiction and futuristic bio-technological hybrids.

▶ [mowax.com] Animated blobs on the web site of the record label Mo'Wax hide the links to the rest of its pages but the site also gives the user an obvious and straight forward, easy selection via a pull-down menu.

[northcreative.com] Design agency North Creative gives users choices of how to get around its site. The option of a 'quick nav' bar is supplied as an alternative to traversing a red Flash-animated globe in which links to the different sections of the site are embedded.

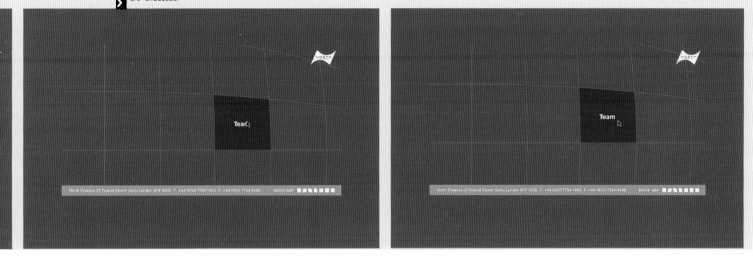

different reasons. Ali Peate, design director of Getfrank, explains that the first is based around a database the broadcaster built up and so up to four different ways of accessing the information have been provided. Gorillaz is even more intuitive as the site is animated and effectively designed to represent the band's home and workplace. So clicking symbolic objects gets you into another part of the web site.

In addition to the choice of navigation tools and ideas, the layout of the site is key. Perhaps the most important consideration is the home page, often called the most valuable piece of real estate in the world. Here, the temptation is to cram in a reference and a link to all of the content on the site. Most users, however, do not want to come under a barrage of information as soon as they enter. Creating hierarchies of information that the user can explore either by clicking through to new pages, or by devices such as drop-down menus, is one solution.

In the US, certainly, Bluewave's Dagny Pieto sees a trend towards an increasingly direct approach in design: 'There's a real push towards utility and simplicity in American web design. There is a big push to simplify. It is task-orientated. You want to pay a bill, for example, and there's a real push to do it in the simplest and most direct way possible.'

In her mind this ties in with a general lifestyle trend for so-called 'simple living' (à la Real Simple magazine, at realsimple.com). She explains: 'People want function without getting too bogged down in the details.' This is carried on to the web guidelines that Bluewave has taken into the corporate arena. 'We've been doing a lot of web guidelines for mega-corporations with multiple sites,' adds Pieto. 'A good example of this is the Exxon-Mobil sites. There are many, many different sites for many, many different audiences, but they all have to follow the guidelines we created for them.' She claims: 'It has really made a difference in their communications – you can always tell you're at an Exxon site. The guidelines are loose enough that the sites can be localized (in language and culture) and made appealing to the targeted user, but tight enough that there is an apparent connection between all Exxon sites.'

[mak.frankfurt.de] The web site of the Museum für Angewandte Kunst Frankfurt am Main in Germany uses a grid of squares as a navigation system. Rolling the cursor over a line of coloured bars at the base of the page activates the squares, allowing the user to select a destination and click through.

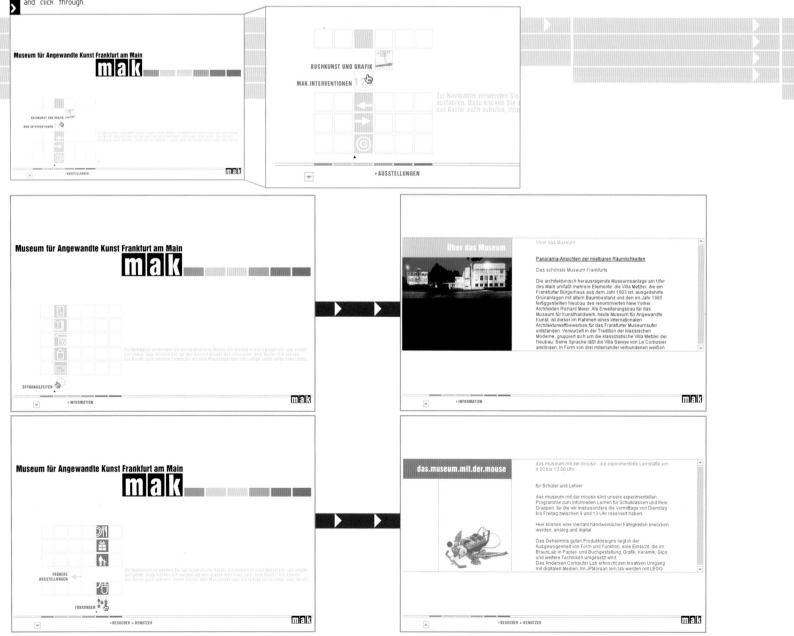

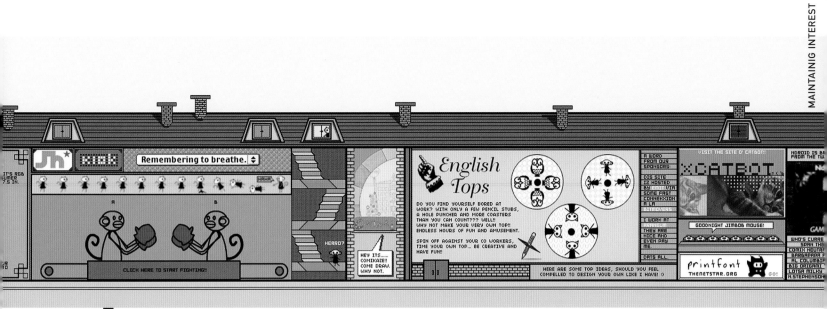

[ndroid.com] Conventional rules — such as those dictating that users do not want to scroll through the page to find what they want, or that scrolling should be vertical — can be broken when the designer assumes a level of sophistication and willingness to experiment on the part of the user, as in this case where the site's content is arranged in the form of a horizontal street.

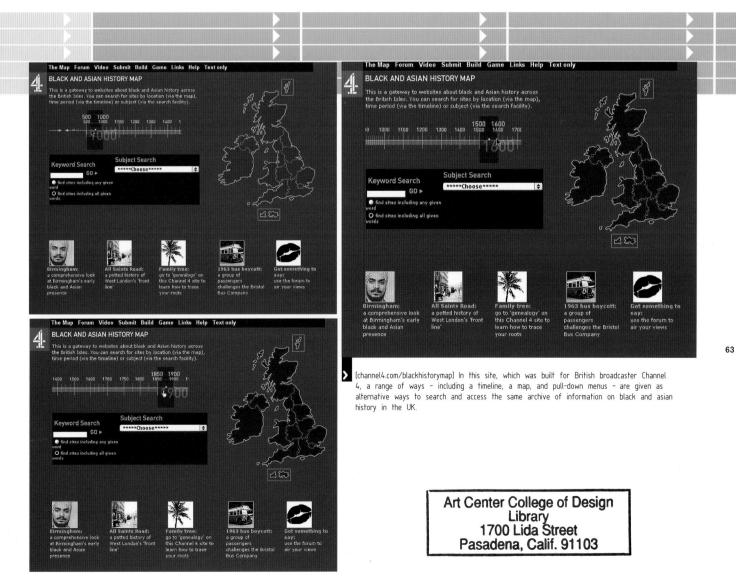

[channel4.com/blackhistorymap] In this site, which was built for British broadcaster Channel 4, a range of ways — including a timeline, a map, and pull-down menus — are given as alternative ways to search and access the same archive of information on black and asian history in the UK.

63

MAINTAINING INTEREST **NAVIGATION**

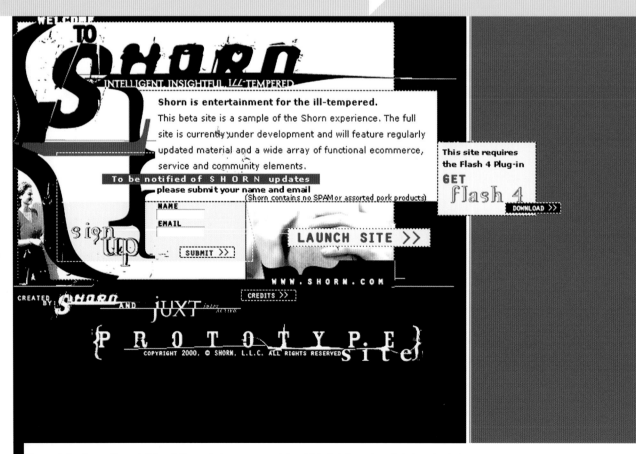

[shorn.com] The typographic pyrotechnics of Shorn.com's homepage suggest immediately that the audience it is interested in is open to experiment.

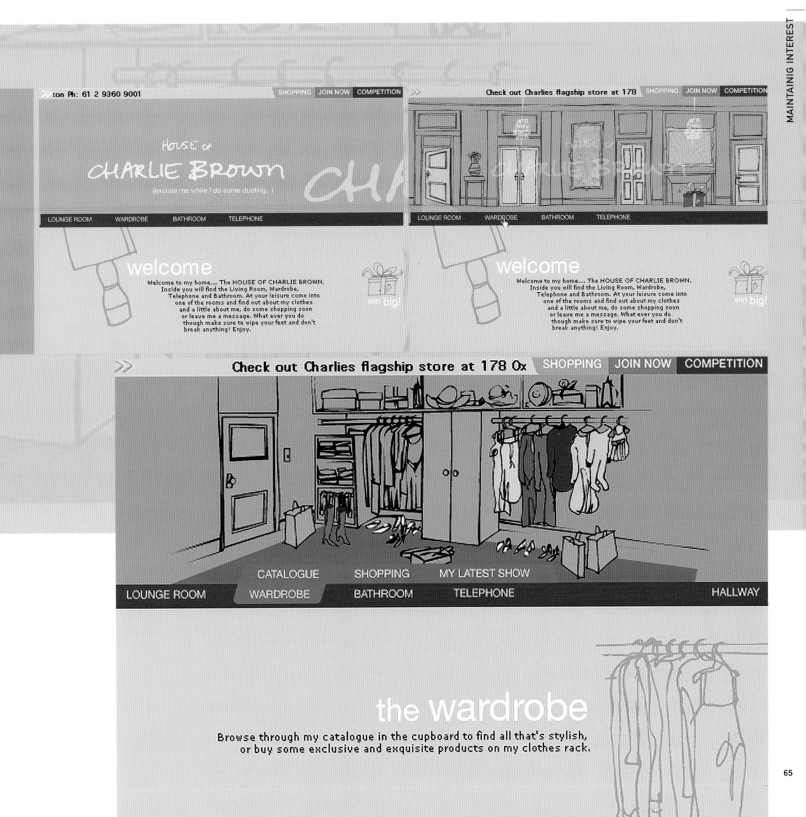

ton Ph: 61 2 9360 9001   SHOPPING JOIN NOW COMPETITION

House of
CHARLIE BROWN
(excuse me while I do some dusting...)

LOUNGE ROOM   WARDROBE   BATHROOM   TELEPHONE

welcome

Welcome to my home.... The HOUSE OF CHARLIE BROWN.
Inside you will find the Living Room, Wardrobe,
Telephone and Bathroom. At your leisure come into
one of the rooms and find out about my clothes
and a little about me, do some shopping soon
or leave me a message. What ever you do
though make sure to wipe your feet and don't
break anything! Enjoy.

win big!

Check out Charlies flagship store at 178   SHOPPING JOIN NOW COMPETITION

LOUNGE ROOM   WARDROBE   BATHROOM   TELEPHONE

welcome

Welcome to my home.... The HOUSE OF CHARLIE BROWN.
Inside you will find the Living Room, Wardrobe,
Telephone and Bathroom. At your leisure come into
one of the rooms and find out about my clothes
and a little about me, do some shopping soon
or leave me a message. What ever you do
though make sure to wipe your feet and don't
break anything! Enjoy.

win big!

Check out Charlies flagship store at 178 Ox   SHOPPING JOIN NOW COMPETITION

CATALOGUE   SHOPPING   MY LATEST SHOW

LOUNGE ROOM   WARDROBE   BATHROOM   TELEPHONE   HALLWAY

the wardrobe

Browse through my catalogue in the cupboard to find all that's stylish,
or buy some exclusive and exquisite products on my clothes rack.

> [charliebrownonline.com] The web site of this clothing retailer is designed as a store, where access to the different areas of the site is, as one would expect, via doors, and products hang on rails. While the navigation system is comparatively unusual, because it is based on real world experience, it is immediately comprehensible.

MAINTAINING INTEREST **PSYCHOLOGY & CULTURE**

One of the problems with the way that designers expect users to behave on web sites is that they do not necessarily understand how a user thinks in relation to technology. Then even if the problem is understood correctly, it needs to be acted on.

Dr Dan Brown, a doctor of psychology at Applied Psychology Research, which looks at the relationship between shoppers and retailers online and off, praises the way that Amazon presents buying lists to its users. 'It does demand empathy. If it says "here are 10 books you might want to read" and you already know three or four of them then you will feel it is on to something,' he says. Sites ask users to do different things than they are used to doing in the offline world and design can help them get used to this. By way of example, Brown suggests that the number and variety of products stocked by most e-tailers is many times that of offline equivalents. 'No individual shop offers, and no individual customer normally faces that level of choice, so the user needs to be presented with an adequate search engine which allows them to search in a fluid way.'

Not only do different people have different ideas, but different cultural groups – both geographic and demographic – do not look at web sites for the same features or functions or in the same way. Andy Smith, research director at usability company optimum.web explains: 'You first need to understand effective human-to-human

communication in a particular cultural context and then build systems to match. Clearly the way people communicate varies considerably across countries and cultures.'

Dagny Pieto of Bluewave in New York says that Microsoft has looked carefully at localising its corporate site for different countries, and by extension taken into account different cultures. Ross Stewart, art director for Bluewave Asia Pacific, notes that one of the big cultural factors in site design in Asia is the use of colour. Red is associated with the Chinese New Year and aspects of money and finance. So it might be used appropriately on a banking web site: 'It's positive to use because people in some countries are used to it and it will be used in a positive connection.'

In Hong Kong or Japan there are expectations that sites have as much activity, graphics and content as possible. 'Neon signs everywhere and sites which have bells and whistles,' says Ross Stewart. 'Europeans might see it as corny as hell but it is expected there.' However, even such broad generalisations can be misleading, when what is required is a forensic understanding of a particular culture. Ross Stewart cites the example of designing a site for Taiwan, which has a relatively new audience online, compared to the more sophisticated market of Japan. 'In Japan, we understand that a click on a logo in the top left-hand corner of a page should take you through to the relevant homepage.

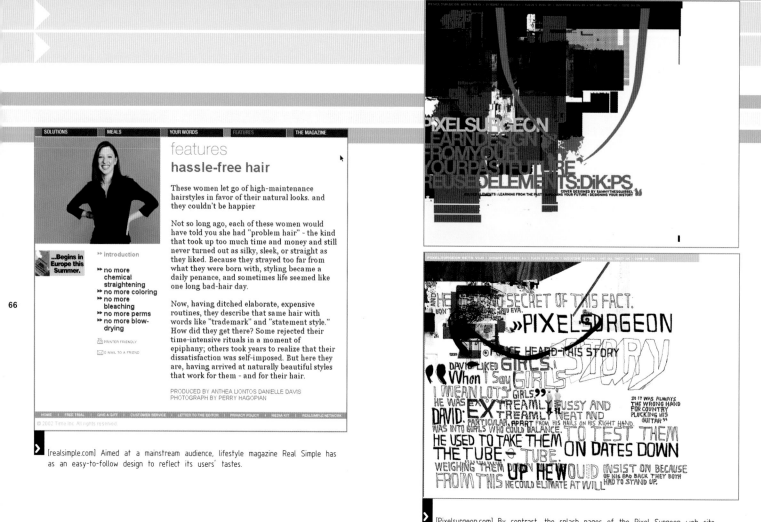

[realsimple.com] Aimed at a mainstream audience, lifestyle magazine Real Simple has as an easy-to-follow design to reflect its users' tastes.

[Pixelsurgeon.com] By contrast, the splash pages of the Pixel Surgeon web site, which are changed regularly, consciously break many of the 'rules' of graphic design in the knowledge that its audience is visually sophisticated enough to appreciate it. These pages were designed by Design is Kinky (top) and Neasden ControlCentre (below).

This is not necessarily the understanding of a user in Taiwan. Users do not necessarily understand the shorthand we assume they do.'

Awareness of local differences is also crucial. This can include the straightforward difference between a site that is aiming to get consumers interested or one that is looking to get a business audience interested. Naturally the consumer may be attracted by the very features – bright colours, animations, pictures – which might look frivolous to a business audience. However the potential audience is split or segmented – by age, profession, geographical location – and this should also be borne in mind.

[microsoft.hk] Microsoft's homepage in Hong Kong places a different emphasis on images, for example, while still following the corporate template.

[microsoft.com] Software giant Microsoft has been singled out for its attention-to-detail in localising its many country sites. This is its US hub.

Blind and partially sighted people can have problems using many web sites, in particular, because many design features can be confusing. And if web sites do not cater for that sector of the population, they miss out on large volumes of potential   users: in the UK alone, up to two million people have serious sight problems.

This is being highlighted – not least by the US-based World-Wide Web Consortium (W3C), the body that establishes standards for the web – and many commercial organisations are realising that they can ensure that their web sites can be accessible to all of the population, not just the fully sighted.

In Britain, the charity Royal National Institute for the Blind (RNIB) promotes the idea of accessible sites – with the growth of synthesised speech and Braille display technology, it says, even the completely blind can use the web. First, it recommends that the site is written in valid html code. 'The web is an information medium but too many web designers still think of it as a purely visual medium and are unaware even that visually impaired people can access the web,' says Julie Howells, the RNIB's campaigns officer for access to digital information.

Although people with sight problems have different needs and circumstances, most require a highly contrasting colour scheme.

In July 2001, Aspect Internet – which offers an accessibility development service for web sites – conducted a survey which found that the vast majority even of the top listed companies on the UK stock exchange failed to meet basic criteria for accessible site design. Jon Russell, commercial director of Aspect Internet, said: 'Neglect of the disabled is shameful in any form but I believe this is primarily due to a lack of awareness. The tools are out there to remedy this situation; it's simply a matter of being aware that they exist.'

Problems Aspect noted in the survey included use of small type and poorly contrasting colours – a quarter of the sites did not meet colour contrast standards. Some 62 per cent were 'virtually' useless when viewed in a text-only format.

Other forms of disability were not necessarily catered for either. Russell notes that for people who have difficulty using a mouse – those with motor disabilities, say – it would mean that many of those sites were inaccessible.

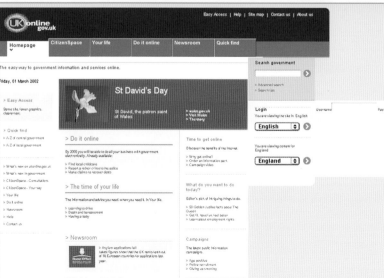

[ukonline.gov.uk] The British Government's initiative to get the UK online has an easy access version which it explains is the 'same site, fewer graphics, clearer text'.

[websavvy-access.org] Sample accessible pages by Web-Savvy, a firm which advises sites on accessibility issues.

[saga.co.uk] In an attempt to reflect the tastes and preferences of an older audience, Saga clearly highlights its different strengths – from health to travel – on its home page. As it is aimed at an older audience it uses larger typefaces and an uncluttered and straightforward design

The RNIB gives a mark of approved accessible sites, the 'See it Right Accessible Website'. To date the Royal Mail and Standard Life Investments sites have this mark awarded. A big breakthrough in the acknowledgement of the importance of providing and designing web sites for the disabled was the decision by UK supermarket giant Tesco to launch a section for the disabled on its grocery shopping site.

Tesco, which is working with Safeway Inc. in the USA, launched a standalone version of its original site called the Tesco Access Grocery Service. It uses voice software and has a basic text construction and only has basic html-scripting and single-frame construction. Tesco can still offer its entire product range on the site – it is not just a stripped down version of its main online store.

Ironically, anecdotal evidence suggests that some fully sighted users shop on Tesco Access because it is so easy to use. All populations in the West are ageing – some reports suggest that within a few years, half the population will be of pensionable age – and the over 50s have also been one of the keenest convert groups to the web. Site owners and designers cannot afford not to accommodate the requirements of these groups.

MAINTAINING INTEREST **ENTERTAINMENT**

Sites have got to work functionally and technically, yes, and one of the bigger areas of investment online – though it is a moot point about how effective that spend has been in a lot of cases – is in the corporate information sector, but plenty of sites aim just to entertain. This can be by featuring irreverent or gossipy content, use of rich-media or audio and visual content, or simply by adding gaming content.

One of the sectors that saw the most enthusiasm and growth online in the last couple of years was gaming. Some sites like Uproar and Flipside are totally designed for games. But the provision of free entertainment on sites whose purposes range from brand-building to retail is one of the key ways that owners encourage visitors to dwell at their sites, make repeat visits and recommend them to their friends.

In themselves, games can be used to provide information about brands and products in a way that is palatable and appealing to the site visitor. Owners of Fast Moving Consumer Goods (FMCGs)

like soft drinks or chocolate bars have embraced the web. A site about chocolate or soft drinks may not in itself attract or maintain much traffic, but providing entertainment has been a key way for them to entice users to interact with the brand. Bruce Thomas, founder of web design agency Subnetactive, has worked on sites for FMCG brands such as Kelloggs' breakfast cereal Frosties. He points out that some games may well be designed for children, but they are not just played by kids. Designed by Magnetic North, the Frosties.co.uk site talks to the user – it is aimed at young kids – as if they are interacting with Tony the Tiger himself. The animated home page gives clues so that children can find a 'secret' area on the web site. Once there, Tony briefs them on how to help him join a secret organisation to fight his arch-foe Dr Cheetah and 'pour cold milk' on his evil plans. Another Kelloggs' site Magnetic North has worked on is Uder.co.uk, for its Cereal and Milk snack bars. Users sign up as detectives to help Uder the animated cow solve crimes, or go back in time to find a dragon. Naturally, this game involves pouring cold milk on a dragon.

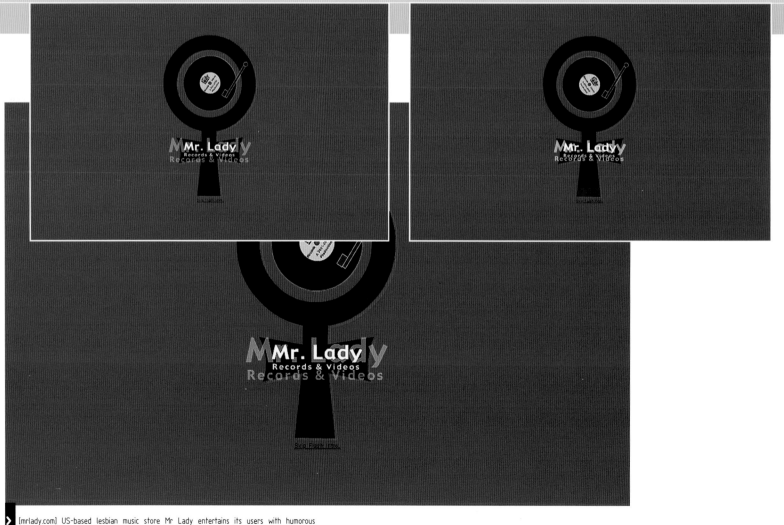

▶ [mrlady.com] US-based lesbian music store Mr Lady entertains its users with humorous 'homoscopes' which gives it a distinctive personality.

Other forms of entertainment popular on web sites include those familiar from consumer magazines, from crosswords to horoscopes, as well as humorous writing and opportunities for the user to interact with the site through tests and quizzes, or by contributing their own content.

71

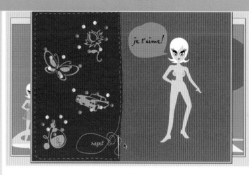

> [lilyhats.com] San Francisco-based hat maker Lily Fighera gives shoppers the chance to try out hat and clothing combinations on a model figure before they go shopping.

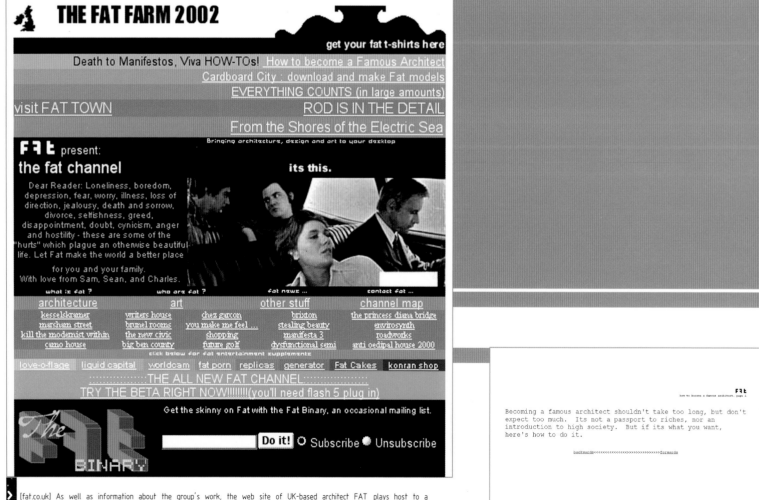

> [fat.co.uk] As well as information about the group's work, the web site of UK-based architect FAT plays host to a wide variety of highly entertaining but unusual content, including a tongue-in-cheek 14 step guide to becoming a famous architect, and a selection of cakes in the shape of unappetising buildings, such as a nuclear power plant and an arms dump.

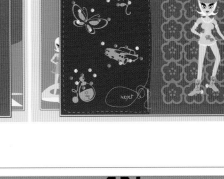

cake stall: **russian radar station**

book   iraqi arms   dealey   sellafield   united   russian radar   the

...y a visit to any well stocked newsagent. Buy one
...each design magazine. You will use these to find out
... to do.

backwards<<<<<<<<<<<<<<>>>>>>>>>>>>>forwards

Now go to your local remaindered book store. Buy a copy of a
design book with lots of pictures in. Not only is the
remaindered store cheaper, but its stock is between ten to
fifteen years old. These are the least fashionable and so most
shocking of all styles. You will use this to copy your new
designs from.

backwards<<<<<<<<<<<<<<>>>>>>>>>>>>>forwards

Now its time to develop your mystique. This is all important,
because it is what you are selling. Remember, you won't have
to design a building for at least ten years. And in this time
you will live off your mystique, so make it good. Mystique is
what you say, and the way that you say it. If you come from
continental Europe, great. If you don't, pretend that you do.
Mystique should also suggest revolutionary politics and french
philosophy. Don't talk about these things directly as it
never makes good copy and will only confuse you.

backwards<<<<<<<<<<<<<<>>>>>>>>>>>>>forwards

_MAINTAINING INTEREST ENTERTAINMENT

One problem that sites which use games encounter is the temptation to use the most advanced technology possible which can cause lengthy download times for users, even though they have the correct plug-ins. However, simple games have worked effectively as a way to expose users to a brand or advertising as part of a larger web site.

Christian Guthier, creative director of online gaming platform provider Hi2 Ltd, has worked for a number of European ISPs, from pan-European Tiscali to the UK's Freeserve, helping them add gaming content. He says that the issues posed by designing games for portals are different to those faced by stand-alone gaming sites. The site of an Internet Service Provider, for example, will not want to alienate existing users by introducing something that is too over the top and obtrusive. It also wants to offer something accessible to those new users, who are not experienced online game players, when they explore the site before venturing out to the rest of the web. However, as Gruthier notes, 'Online gamers tend to be very loyal once 'hooked' on to a product or site.'

74

▶ [threadless.com] For a limited period, visitors to the site of online clothing retailer threadless.com were surprised to find the homepage upside down. A single click on the page turned it the right way up. This was, it seems, an amusing play on the common web experience of finding so many broken links, server errors and other technical obstructions while surfing some sites that the user begins to wonder if there is a human organization behind them at all. The human quality of Threadless is plain to see from this prank.

[uder.co.uk] The web site of Kellogg's Cereal and Milk Bars encourages users to interact with the brand through the provision of games.

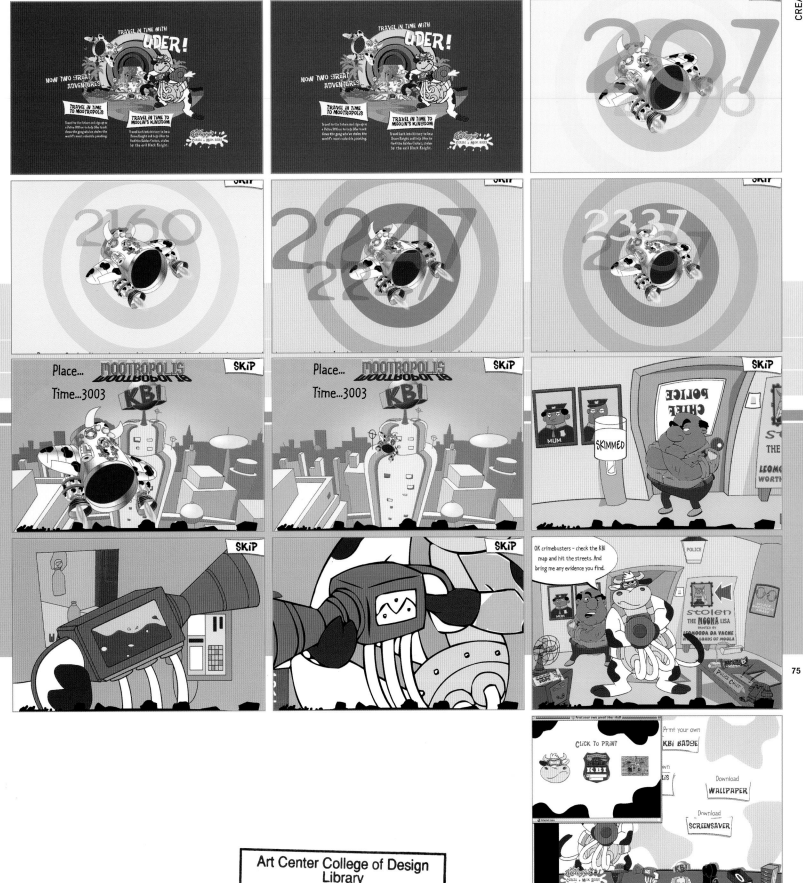

75

MAINTAINING INTEREST **CONTENT**

Naturally 'content' comes in many shapes and sizes – there are almost as many types as there are web sites – from news, reviews and feature articles to galleries, sound archives and even web cams. The idea, which gave rise to the oft-quoted and oft-ridiculed online business maxim that 'content is king', is that whatever the business of a web site – from e-commerce to a corporate brochure online – added 'content' will encourage users to visit, to stay longer, to explore further, and to return for updates. Good content boosts the brand and that in turn boosts the site's fortune. If the content is updated and 'sticky' enough, users and viewers will want to return to the site, not just once, but to make it a regular destination. Ultimately, good content helps the site fulfil its ambitions and should – once promoted – become a self-fulfilling prophecy.

The designer's role is not simply to showcase content, but to devise content – to behave like the editor of a magazine or the director of a TV show. They must ensure that content is appropriate, and make editorial judgements about how content might support the aims of the site – whether that be selling products or services, or providing corporate information – without sounding like advertising; visitors are unlikely to want to read blatantly promotional copy.

Like most things, creating good content is easier said than done. One factor is that content can cost and it is that knowledge which fuelled the race for content-driven sites to open up revenue streams other than just relying on online advertising. Amazon, on the other hand, is obviously primarily an e-commerce site, but the content it contains – book reviews by site users – is central to its appeal. And not only do the reviews have the all important impartiality, they are, after administration costs, free to Amazon as the content is provided by site users. This is an increasingly popular model for sites whose users want to find content, and are more than happy to contribute to it themselves.

Even the most straightforward content, as featured on news and information sites, which is text-based, poses its own problems. Alasdair Scott, creative director of web design consultancy Arnold Interactive, notes that initially a lot of information sites mimicked

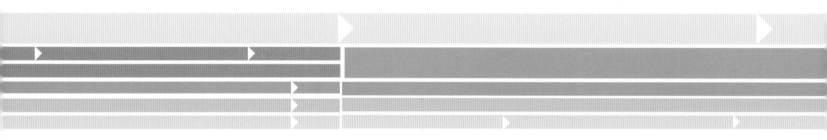

[ferrisplock.com] The 'Sightings' section of site the American designer Ferris Plock contains submissions by visitors – a useful way to gather content and one that allows visitors to feel that they have a stake in the site.

ferris plock productions

news

here's hoping everyone had a rocking saint patrick's and is recuperating nicely.

ferris plock tees are now available in the fabulous castro → at Get Ups, castro and 19th.

hate leaving your house? dying to get a ferris plock tee? **gearmonkey.com** can help.

ferris plock productions

sightings

if you have a fpp related picture and you want it posted on the site **send it** and we will check it out. refresh your screen for a new image.

home
about ferris
designs
merchandise
sightings
links
contact
stickers

MAINTAINING INTEREST CONTENT

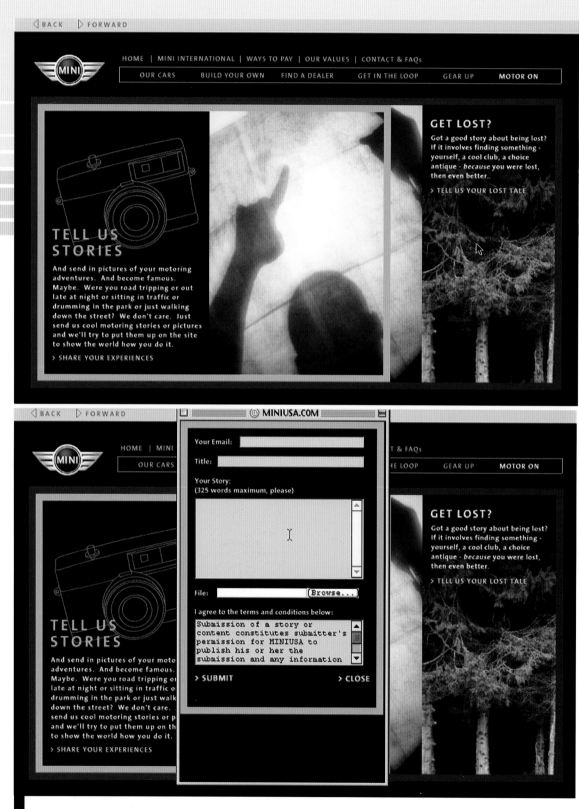

[miniusa.com] Based on themes developed in Mini's offline advertising, the US site for the popular small car asks visitors to tell their own stories and share their Mini-based experiences and tales.

their offline counterparts. For instance, the online offshoot of a newspaper looks like the front page of a broadsheet that has been put on a screen. Likewise, broadcasters' web sites initially tried to do what was done on TV.

This may pander to the audience's expectations but each medium has its own strengths, and it certainly sells some of the opportunities for interaction – unique to digital media – short. For instance, a news story can have embedded links to other stories giving context and background to a piece. Users can be encouraged to email the writer. As Alasdair Scott says, 'Initially content driven sites assumed that the web was effectively the digital version of a magazine or a TV programme. The first range of sites assumed that users wanted just the same amount of

information as they got from other media. They actually want much more.' And now, as the user has got more sophisticated, they expect it. As Scott notes, a lot of publishers' web sites have a searchable archive of past stories as a fundamental feature.

And just as making past content available is a cheap and easy way to build valuable volumes of material, so it is useful to make clear on the site when updates are due. While it is unlikely that visitors will make a note of the date and return then, they will register the fact that the site is not static, and may browse it again in the expectation of seeing something new.

[twice2.ch] Visitors to this Swiss design site are greeted by a pop-up window detailing the latest news. By making such a distinctive feature of the news page, the designers ensure that visitors realise that content is regularly updated..

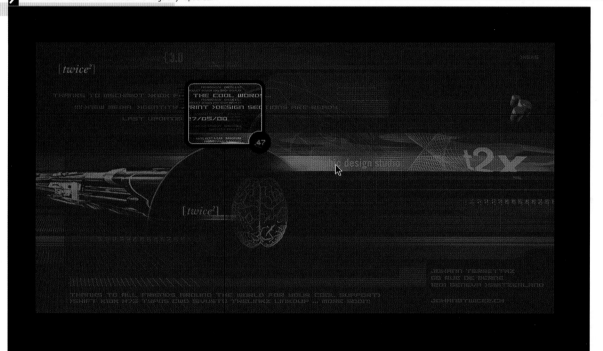

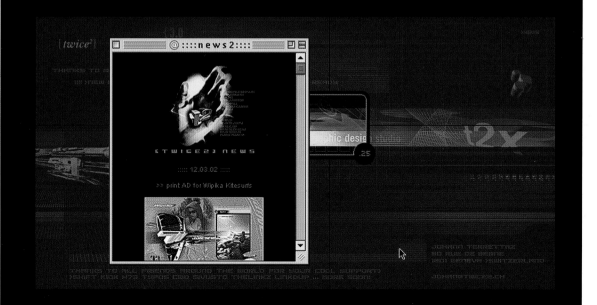

MAINTAINING INTEREST REDESIGN

Rarely is the first incarnation of a web site the finished product. It sometimes appears that the launch of a site is merely the start to an on-going process of updates, change and development, beginning with the tweaks and changes made after a 'soft launch', where a trial version of the site is tested for bugs and glitches.

Redesigns usually take place either when feedback shows the existing format isn't working, or just to keep the site a fresh and exciting place to visit. Web design moves fast, and even the newest sites can quickly begin to look out of date, as well as feeling stale to regular visitors.

In the latter instance, there are two possible approaches: the complete overhaul, in which the old site is scrapped and replaced with an entirely new one, or a more subtle revamp of the type known in the UK as the 'Marmite' approach, after the packaging of the long established sandwich spread which customers believe to be the same it always has been because of the incremental way it has been updated and refined over decades. The Marmite approach is useful in maintaining brand loyalty and awareness while keeping up-to-date. Sites such as Sports.com and Degriftour.com have gradually evolved their design to reflect the incorporation of new ideas and revenue streams.

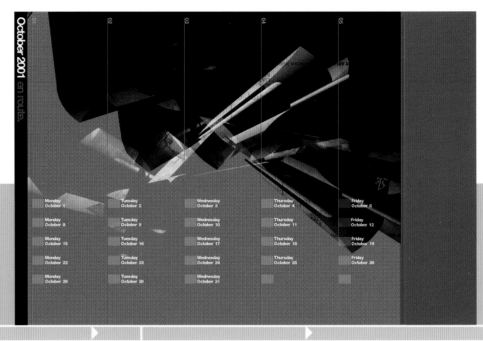

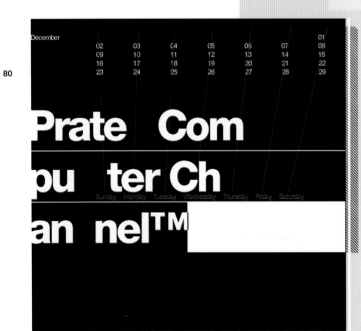

Web sites are often compared to offline equivalents – whether that be in media or in retail. Print magazines keep the framework of their design – typeface, grid and so on – from month to month, but change everything else: layouts, colours, and perhaps most important, cover image. Likewise, while most shops are only completely refitted every few years, they change their window displays, and their product displays. Web sites can learn lessons from these offline equivalents in keeping the design consistent – to ensure recognition – but fresh enough to encourage consumers to return. Many sites, therefore, update their appearance simply to keep them fresh and capitalise on changing fashions and attitudes in their audience. It also means that the site has the opportunity to keep up with advances in technology and to maintain its efficiency and user-friendliness.

Some redesigns, however, are the result of fundamental changes in business strategy or changes in ownership, but even when this is the case, there is often the opportunity to incorporate responses to feedback about what keeps users interested.

> [prate.com] Prate.com acts as an online calendar, with a different design for each month.

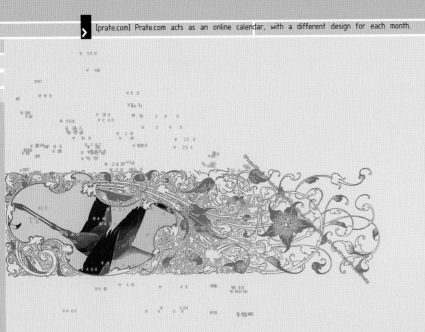

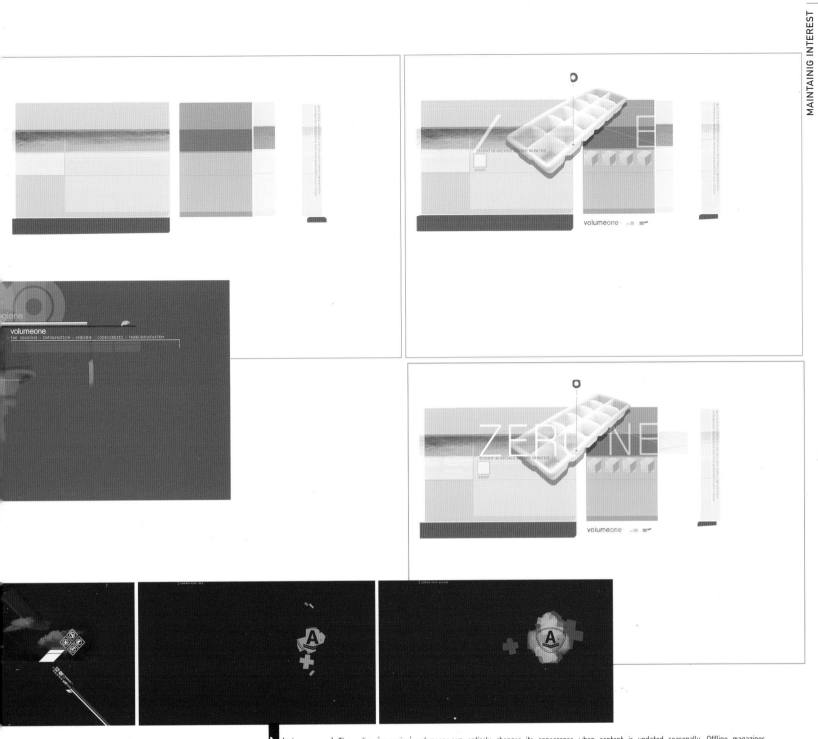

> [volumeone.com] The online 'magazine' volumeone.com entirely changes its appearance when content is updated seasonally. Offline magazines rarely change every aspect of their design with each issue, but do change the cover, not least to let readers know that there is a new issue on the shelves. Web sites, similarly, can change their design to let regular browsers know that content has been updated.

02

MAINTAINING INTEREST THE RETAIL EXPERIENCE

Retailers online share a single aim – they want users to buy from their web site and, provided the correct fulfilment operation is in place, get the goods they want so that they will return and repeat the process. Second best is that users' purchasing decisions offline are prompted by a store or brand owner's own web site, even if the transaction itself does not happen on line – according to researcher Jupiter Media Metrix, Internet-generated (as opposed to online) car sales could jump to 32 per cent of total new car sales by 2006 from 13 per cent world-wide in 2001.

How the e-tailer takes the customer to the point where they wish to make a purchase can be done in an almost infinite number of ways, but the key to success is to provide a satisfying retail experience, that begins the moment the user enters the site, and continues through delivery of the product, to the next time they return to the site and onwards. In anticipation of such repeat business, sites like online book and music retailers Amazon.com and Bol.com – Bertelsmann's primarily European-based e-tailing equivalent – now offer personalisation.

Partly this is facilitated by technologies such as cookies, partly by the customer informing the site of their preferences. This presumes that the customer is prepared to make further purchases and already expects the brand to offer the expertise as well as the inventory to effectively recommend products.

Not only do e-commerce sites target a range of different audiences – from specialist e-tailer Firebox.com, which offers gadgets and boys' toys and games to youth with disposable income, to the online offshoots of traditional retailers such as the American department store Macy's (macys.com) – but they also have to bear in mind, as do most online outlets, that the online audience is changing too. In the last two years the demographics of the web have changed dramatically, with the addition of large numbers of female users, and a much broader age range across the potential audience.

It is not an absolute rule to make the purchasing process as quick as possible. For instance, sometimes people not used to the web

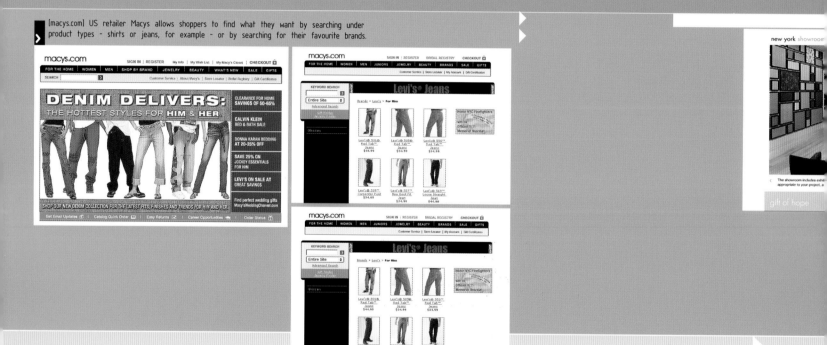

[macys.com] US retailer Macys allows shoppers to find what they want by searching under product types - shirts or jeans, for example - or by searching for their favourite brands.

new york showroom

[xlarge.com] US-based fashion retailer Xlarge.com allows users to design their own retail experience by setting background colours and choosing from a selection of over 40 songs to listen to while they browse.

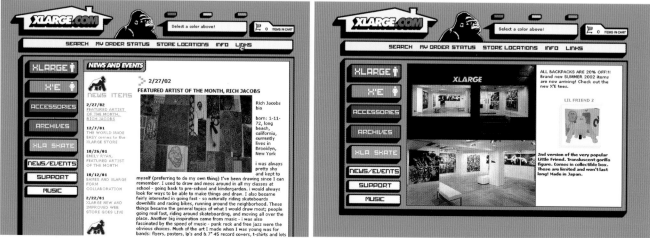

and shopping online may need a few steps in the process to make them feel comfortable with the function and secure with the site, explains Dan Harman, art director of Bluewave UK: 'It is an emotional response and that needs to be catered for.' Many people also like to have as pleasurable an experience while they shop online as they do offline. Others , however, shop online precisely to avoid the rigmarole that offline shopping entails. Designers must be sensitive to both of these extremes.

In some respects, the 'classic' design of a site like Amazon.com has very little reason to change. The nature of the products it sells – such as books and CDs – does not change fundamentally so that it does not need to anticipate making much explanation of each item, apart from, say, mentioning the author and the title of the work. The design of the home page just needs to be flexible enough to showcase the product lines and cope with expansion when the e-tailer introduces a new area of goods, like home computers. And shoppers can either purchase their product with a minimum of fuss, or linger to read reviews, or even post their own.

UK site Firebox.com, which sells a range of weird and wonderful gadgets or boys' toys from shot glass chess sets to table football games, has to straddle this problem. Michael Smith, co-founder and ceo of Firebox.com, explains that there are three types of customers to be catered for by the site. Its design reflects the fact that 'there are people who have never been to the site before, there are those who have been before but may not remember all of the steps or parts of the site and those who visit the site very regularly and just want to know what is new.' The latter spend a lot of money with the site and so, Smith says, should not be alienated. 'So we cater for them by making sure that there is a section of our 20 most recent products on the right hand side of the home page. Other users can chose to disregard that. The key is not to overload them with information,' he adds. Smith feels it is important to offer a range of ways to navigate the site. 'Users can have a very specific product in mind or want to look for a gift or be restricted by the price range. We can show just the latest products or restrict it to what everyone else is buying.'

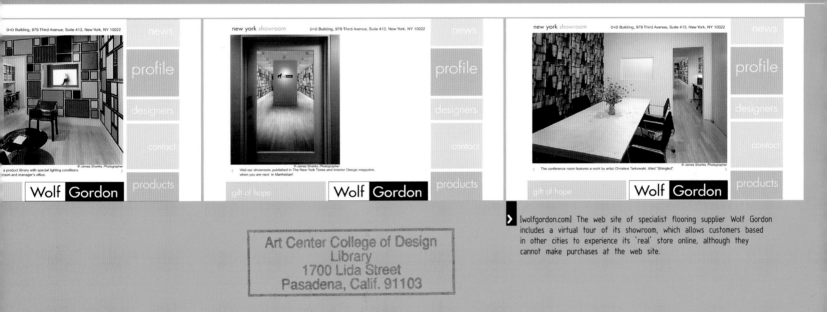

[wolfgordon.com] The web site of specialist flooring supplier Wolf Gordon includes a virtual tour of its showroom, which allows customers based in other cities to experience its 'real' store online, although they cannot make purchases at the web site.

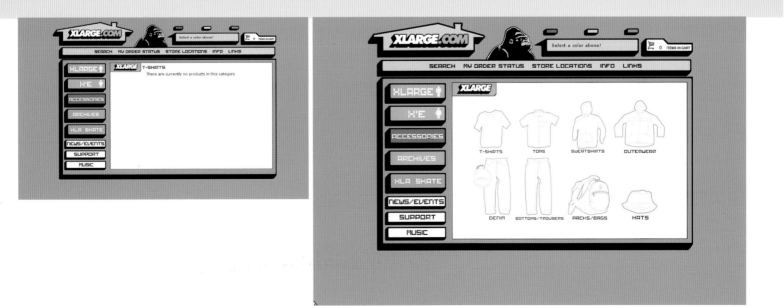

MAINTAINING INTEREST RETAIL & EXPERIENCE

[paulsmith.co.uk] The site of British fashion designer Paul Smith is not primarily designed for e-commerce, although items are occasionally sold through the site. It's main purpose is to create an elegant 'showroom' in keeping with the stylish and aspirational brand. High quality photographs and musical accompaniment contribute to the atmosphere.

Ultimately though there has to be a measure of compromise. 'We sell products that need describing and that needs to be a combination between text and graphics when presented. You are not going to read a lot of information but two photographs at most should sum it up. And including customer reviews gives it another dimension – they are very important. We rely on feedback from our customers.'

According to Chris Cleave, head of customer experience at lastminute.com, the site has to reflect two very separate needs of its customers. Lastminute.com's internal mission statement is to offer consumers 'inspiration and solutions at the last minute'. So it needs to respond to those customers which know what they want down to specific details – a flight for two to Barcelona after 8 O'clock on Friday which will return in time to get to the office by 8 O'clock Monday morning – as well as those who just want to book a holiday for six friends somewhere sunny in July, below a certain price.

Cleave explains that the site features a search engine which should mean customers in the first category are only one click away from what they want. Those in the second have the opportunity to check categories across product verticals under the site's Do Something pages. 'People prefer the site to not been seen to be stable over time – things must change.'

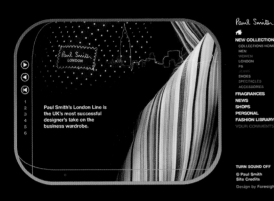

87

COLLECTIONS HOME

MEN

WOMEN

LONDON

PS

JEANS

SHOES

SPECTACLES

ACCESSORIES

FRAGRANCES

NEWS

SHOPS

PERSONAL

FASHION LIBRARY

YOUR COMMENTS

Navy shadow
pinstripe suit with a
blue shadow striped
shirt and blue
patterned tie

TURN SOUND OFF

© **Paul Smith**
Site Credits

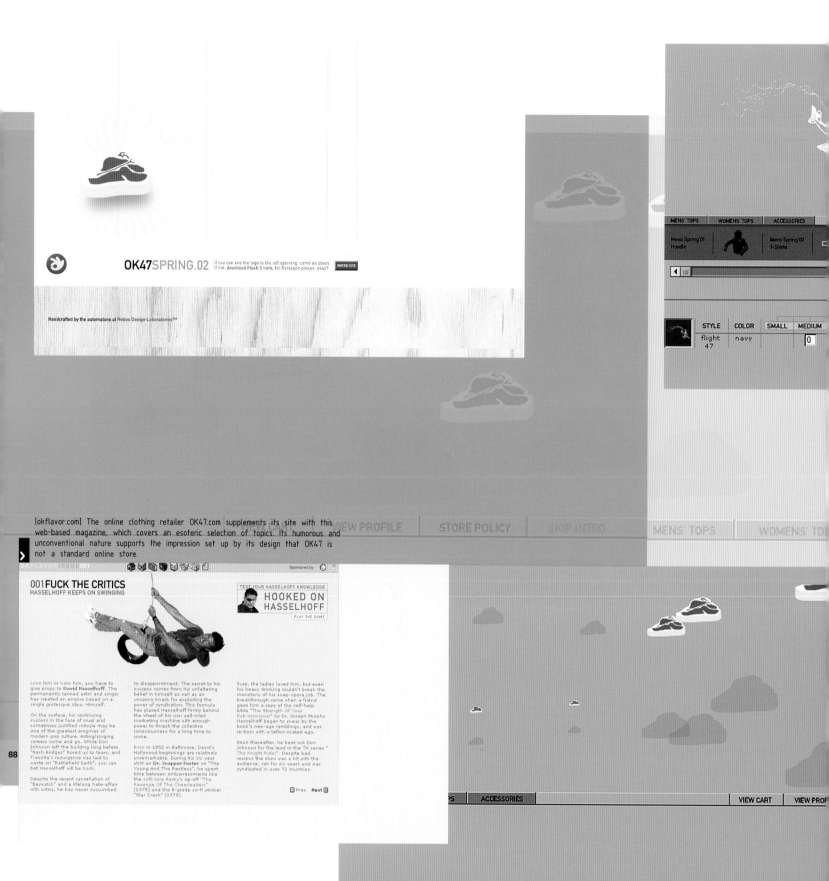

OK47SPRING.02   If you can see the logo to the left spinning, come on down. If not, download Flash 5 here. No Netscape please, okay?   ENTER SITE

Handcrafted by the automatons at Helios Design Laboratories™

MENS' TOPS   WOMENS' TOPS   ACCESSORIES

Mens Spring 01   Mens Spring 02
Hoodie   T-Shirts

	STYLE	COLOR	SMALL	MEDIUM
	flight 47	navy		0

[okflavor.com] The online clothing retailer OK47.com supplements its site with this web-based magazine, which covers an esoteric selection of topics. Its humorous and unconventional nature supports the impression set up by its design that OK47 is not a standard online store.

VIEW PROFILE   STORE POLICY   SKIP INTRO   MENS' TOPS   WOMENS' TO

OKFLAVORISSUE 001   Sponsored by

001FUCK THE CRITICS
HASSELHOFF KEEPS ON SWINGING

TEST YOUR HASSELHOFF KNOWLEDGE

HOOKED ON
HASSELHOFF

PLAY THE GAME

Love him or hate him, you have to give props to **David Hasselhoff**. The permanently tanned actor and singer has created an empire based on a single grotesque idea: Himself.

On the surface, his continuing success in the face of cruel and sometimes justified ridicule may be one of the greatest enigmas of modern pop culture. Acting/singing careers come and go. While Don Johnson left the building long before "Nash Bridges" bored us to tears, and Travolta's resurgence was laid to waste on "Battlefield Earth", you can bet Hasselhoff will be back.

Despite the recent cancellation of "Baywatch" and a lifelong hate-affair with critics, he has never succumbed

to disappointment. The secret to his success comes from his unfaltering belief in himself as well as an uncanny knack for exploiting the power of syndication. This formula has placed Hasselhoff firmly behind the wheel of his own well-oiled marketing machine with enough power to thrash the collective consciousness for a long time to come.

Born in 1952 in Baltimore, David's Hollywood beginnings are relatively unremarkable. During his six year stint as **Dr. Snapper Foster** on "The Young And The Restless", he spent time between embarrassments like the soft-core Porky's rip-off "The Revenge Of The Cheerleaders" (1975) and the B-grade sci-fi stinker "Star Crash" (1979).

Sure, the ladies loved him, but even his heavy drinking couldn't break the monotony of his soap-opera job. The breakthrough came when a friend gave him a copy of the self-help bible "The Strength Of Your Sub-conscious" by Dr. Joseph Murphy. Hasselhoff began to swear by the book's new-age ramblings, and was re-born with a teflon-coated ego.

Soon thereafter, he beat out Don Johnson for the lead in the TV series "The Knight Rider". Despite bad reviews the show was a hit with the audience, ran for six years and was syndicated in over 72 countries.

◁ Prev   Next ▷

PS   ACCESSORIES   VIEW CART   VIEW PROF

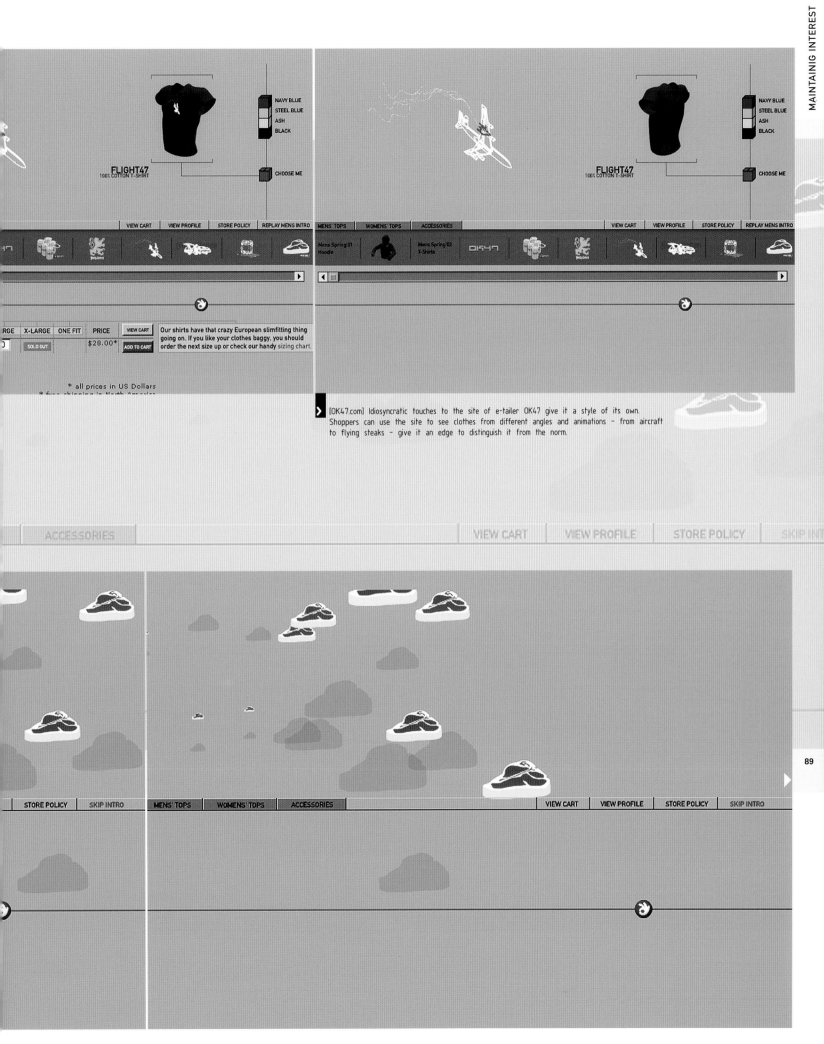

FLIGHT47
100% COTTON T-SHIRT

NAVY BLUE
STEEL BLUE
ASH
BLACK

CHOOSE ME

FLIGHT47
100% COTTON T-SHIRT

NAVY BLUE
STEEL BLUE
ASH
BLACK

CHOOSE ME

VIEW CART   VIEW PROFILE   STORE POLICY   REPLAY MENS INTRO

MENS' TOPS   WOMENS' TOPS   ACCESSORIES

Mens Spring/01 Hoodie   Mens Spring/02 T-Shirts   OK47

VIEW CART   VIEW PROFILE   STORE POLICY   REPLAY MENS INTRO

RGE | X-LARGE | ONE FIT | PRICE
SOLD OUT | | | $28.00*

VIEW CART
ADD TO CART

Our shirts have that crazy European slimfitting thing going on. If you like your clothes baggy, you should order the next size up or check our handy sizing chart.

* all prices in US Dollars

[OK47.com] Idiosyncratic touches to the site of e-tailer OK47 give it a style of its own. Shoppers can use the site to see clothes from different angles and animations – from aircraft to flying steaks – give it an edge to distinguish it from the norm.

ACCESSORIES   VIEW CART   VIEW PROFILE   STORE POLICY   SKIP INT

STORE POLICY   SKIP INTRO   MENS' TOPS   WOMENS' TOPS   ACCESSORIES   VIEW CART   VIEW PROFILE   STORE POLICY   SKIP INTRO

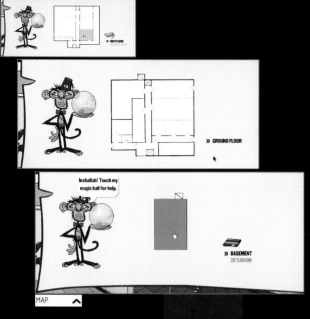

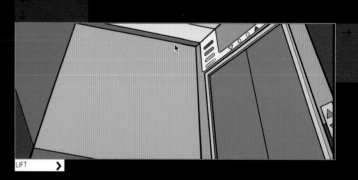

GORRILLA ROOM

With over a million album sales in Europe in just six months, a Platinum album in the UK, a top 20 US hit with 'Clint Eastwood', videos on heavy rotation on MTV, and plans afoot for TV and movie spin-offs, Gorillaz are a big success, and seemingly came out of nowhere – which, of course, they did. Because Gorillaz is an animated virtual rock band. Its members – 2-D, Murdoc, Noodle and Russel – and the world in which they live are drawn by cartoonist Jamie Hewlett. And behind them, making the music, are Brit-pop band Blur's lead singer Damon Albarn and members of the Tom Tom Club, among others.

The animated nature of the band – while preventing them from doing the things that normally allow bands to promote themselves and interact with their fans – gave the Gorillaz, and the band's record company EMI, responsible for the marketing, a unique opportunity to create the sort of cross-media, multi-channel success that is increasingly the aim of those in the entertainment industry. And the band's web site, Gorillaz.com, has played a crucial part in that success, which in addition to looking great, courtesy of Hewlett and London-based design group Zombie, is cleverly constructed to encourage exactly the right kind of traffic, and interaction with the band's fans.

The site, which receives around 500,000 hits a month, is promoted off-line, through all of the usual music industry gambits, and it helps, of course, that because the band is animated, the site and music videos are the only places fans can see them move and talk. Capitalising on this, the band premiered the single '19-2000' on the site. Access to games and band information, among other attractions, provides reasons to visit.

91

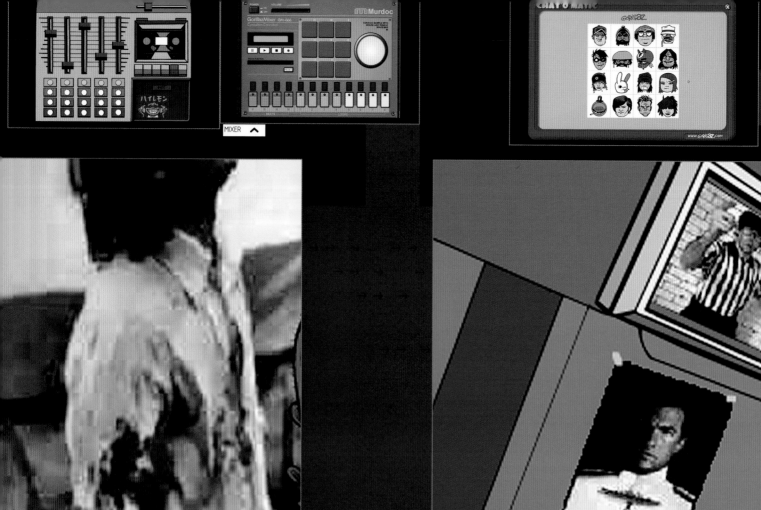

The site design is based around Kong Studios, where the band 'live', rendered in Jamie Hewlett's distinctive cartoon style, and navigation is through rooms of the studio in which various objects act as hidden links to other rooms. This device, which requires some experiment on the part of the user, is appropriate to a band fan site while it may not work so well on a news or e-commerce site. Yet although the site is content rich – with exclusive audio and visual material – it doesn't slow down navigation. The Flash-based intro page can be bypassed and an easily recognisable concept – the web site represents Kong Studios where the band 'lives' and records – means users can get around the different areas easily.

Perhaps the most important decision taken by the client and the designers, however, was to allow the site to become the 'property' of the fans. Most major pop acts frown on fan sites. The attitude seems to be 'Sure fans are nice, but unauthorised material could damage the band's brand'. At Gorillaz.com, on the other hand, in addition to providing a chat room for fans, the site acts as a hub connecting fans through posting links to their own sites. Visiting fans can also remix the band's music on an online five-track machine, and leave their thoughts in the shape of grafitti in the studio's toilets.

Gorillaz

CHAT ROOM

GORILLA ROOM

GORILLA ROOM

GARAGE

GORILLA ROOM

In addition, the band has fully exploited on-line media beyond the confines of its own site to allow users to interact with the site, and share the Gorillaz with friends: Following the band's debut album launch, Yahoo! partnered with MTV Europe to host a global online chat with the band. Viral email campaigns were worked on by design firm Getfrank and label EMI Parlophone.

The use of the web in this way has not only aided the success of the band, but has made its international development possible from a cost perspective: without the web, the Gorillaz could have existed, but would have been a much more expensive proposition. In the early days of the band, at least, the majority of marketing was done through the web site.

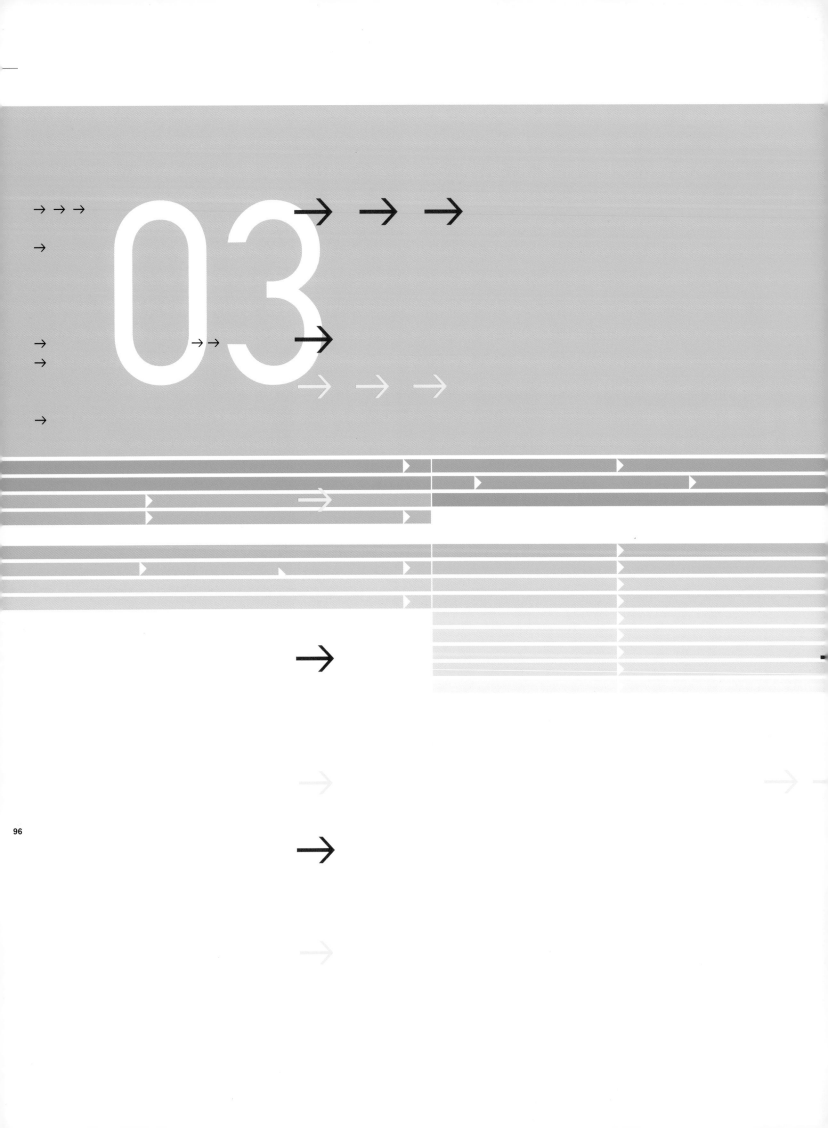

DIRECTING INTEREST

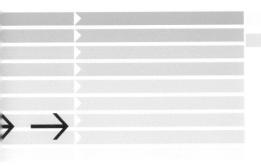

DIRECTING INTEREST INTRODUCTION

At one stage in the development of web sites, particularly amid the dotcom excitement and expectation of 2000, it seemed that all that was required to make money from an online business was to launch the site. It seemed that just providing users with what they wanted would somehow pay for itself and more. More often than not, such ideas promoted the rise of free content sites, and the oft-repeated mantra that 'Content is king'. Sadly, this has proved to be over-optimistic as funding pressures and the realities of the development of the online advertising market (see Chapter One) have resulted in investors and online media owners wanting to see a concrete revenue stream and, often, more than one.

Naturally, this has resulted in changes to the design of web sites as they have wanted to reflect a diversity of activities, or, in some cases, a new focus on the main revenue generating business. In both cases the priority is towards orientating users away from the general content that they can enjoy for free, and towards either the point at which they might decide to make a purchase, or view the specific messages the web site owner wants them to see.

In the former category are sites like sports.com which has placed a firm emphasis on online betting as a revenue stream. Not only is it looking to increase this focus, but it has already introduced a form of badges or flashes into its free content sections which link through to relevant betting pages. Other streams it has introduced include the sale of relevant sports-related merchandise such as personalised team shirts and an SMS alert system, through which the fan is alerted to all goals scored by their team, for a monthly fee. All this, and the continued sale of advertising space on the site, goes to subsidise content which was remains free at the point of consumption.

The British classified advertising site Fish4 has taken the opposite route to reflect its own business model. It now has a very clean cut and focused web page which effectively looks less entertaining at first glance but enables the user to access its core functions offering searches for jobs, cars and property.

Users now generally expect to find a visual balance struck between what they want to view for free, and advertising or links to what the site hopes they will pay for. Users of the software produced by American company Eudora have long been able to get used to this concept. Its email software, available through its web site, has been streamlined into two separate types of product. At the top of the range, its email product is more efficient but users are charged for it. Users can also get a version of this

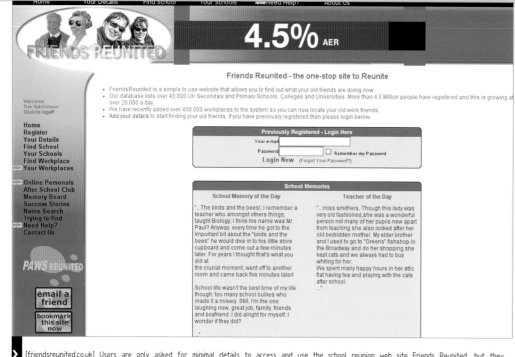

[friendsreunited.co.uk] Users are only asked for minimal details to access and use the school reunion web site Friends Reunited, but they can add further information as they get used to being on the site and want to share details with old school friends

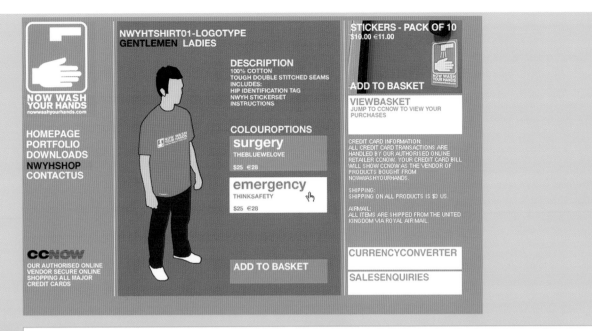

NWYHTSHIRT01-LOGOTYPE
GENTLEMEN LADIES

DESCRIPTION
100% COTTON
TOUGH DOUBLE STITCHED SEAMS
INCLUDES:
HIP IDENTIFICATION TAG
NWYH STICKERSET
INSTRUCTIONS

COLOUROPTIONS

surgery
THEBLUEWELOVE
$25 €28

emergency
THINKSAFETY
$25 €28

ADD TO BASKET

NOW WASH YOUR HANDS
nowwashyourhands.com

HOMEPAGE
PORTFOLIO
DOWNLOADS
NWYHSHOP
CONTACTUS

CCNOW
OUR AUTHORISED ONLINE
VENDOR SECURE ONLINE
SHOPPING ALL MAJOR
CREDIT CARDS

STICKERS - PACK OF 10
$10.00 €11.00

ADD TO BASKET

VIEWBASKET
JUMP TO CCNOW TO VIEW YOUR
PURCHASES

CREDIT CARD INFORMATION:
ALL CREDIT CARD TRANSACTIONS ARE
HANDLED BY OUR AUTHORISED ONLINE
RETAILER CCNOW. YOUR CREDIT CARD BILL
WILL SHOW CCNOW AS THE VENDOR OF
PRODUCTS BOUGHT FROM
NOWWASHYOURHANDS.

SHIPPING:
SHIPPING ON ALL PRODUCTS IS $3 US.

AIRMAIL:
ALL ITEMS ARE SHIPPED FROM THE UNITED
KINGDOM VIA ROYAL AIR MAIL.

CURRENCYCONVERTER

SALESENQUIRIES

CCNow 🛒 ═══════ 🛒 Shopping Cart

NOW WASH YOUR HANDS

Product ID #	Description	Price	Qty
NWYHTEEM	Now Wash Your Hands Tee - Male **Surgery Blue** ⬍ ---- Size ---- ⬍	$25.00	1

Shipping To: Please select here ⬍

Subtotal: $25.00

Packaging and Shipping: $3.00

Grand Total: $28.00

[nowwashyourhands.com] Sites such as Nowwashyourhands are able to have an e-tail aspect by using the services of a specialist online transactions company for payment and fulfilment.

product for free but they have to accept the fact that advertising will be shown to them – effectively subsidising the 'free' product.

Other sites have taken the 'top of the range' approach to the maximum extent and are subscription-only. Such sites should naturally be easier to use and less cluttered, thanks to a smaller reliance on advertising. The Wall Street Journal's online operation has long been held up as an exemplar of this. It even has on its homepage a headline clearly marked 'Free Content'. Naturally, you easily can find out when you are encountering content that it is charging for because you are stopped from going further without the right authorisation, or password, and prompted.

[sports.com] The sports.com content site has been designed to make its content easy-to-read while taking every opportunity to generate revenue by highlighting its betting business and merchandise for sale.

[fish4.co.uk] Users of the Fish4 site are immediately directed to options within its three core areas of job, home and car searches. Although the site brings together classified advertising from 800 different sources, users are not overwhelmed by information as soon as they enter the site.

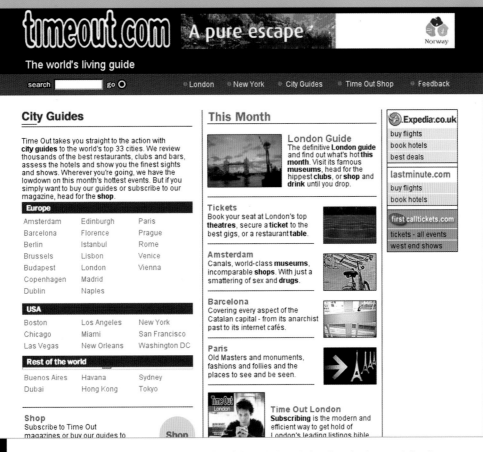

[timeout.com] Online partners of the magazine and guide Time Out are clearly marked on the relevant pages of the site.

101

DIRECTING INTEREST **STRUCTURE**

[volunteermatch.org] This site designed to link volunteers with those who need their help makes the two most important links on the homepage unmissably prominent.

As discussed in Chapter Two, when structuring a web site there are a number of considerations to do with making it navigable and usable, and thereby enhancing the user's experience of the site – they must be able to find what they want and get to it easily. This is of paramount importance: no users, no point in having a site.

But it is also important to consider how the site might be structured in order that the site owner gets what they want from the visit. A site that presents both commercial information and entertainment as a lure for users may not succeed if the two are split so that one can be viewed without any reference to the other. Creating hybrid content, that acts as both brand messaging and entertainment is one solution. Another might be to make sure that not everything the user wants to find is available on the home page – after their interest has been engaged, they will be prepared to click through and find other items of interest. The content and site design must quickly engage interest and build trust, so that the user will explore further.

Perhaps the most fundamental decision the designer makes is what form the site should take. Is it one amorphous blob, or does it effectively work as a number of inter-linked sites, each with its own URL, allowing the site owner to target specific users and present information tailored to them on the home page for example? The form must be determined in part by the users' requirements, but also by those of the site owner: how diverse is the target audience? Will the same pages work for all of them?

What gives a web site its structure, of course, is how the pages are linked together; links between pages, and between sites, are the glue that holds the web together; the essence of what it is about as a medium. Coupled with the use of the back button on the browser, links require one click to take users to a new part of the site, but equally, one click to take them away again. Every time a designer asks a site user to click a link, they risk losing them: the user cannot know for sure what is at the other end, and may lack the patience to find out. This is especially true if they find

FASHION MAGAZINE

CONTENTS
CHIC HAPPENS
LUNCHVOX
JETSETERA
MODEL MANIA
SHOPTART
MESSAGE BOARDS

[hintmag.com] This online fashion publication does not exhaustively describe its contents on the homepage, but instead provides a few intriguing sounding links and one to a contents page.

DIRECTING INTEREST **STRUCTURE**

themselves on what appears to be a never ending quest through the site in search of the content they have been promised. There is a temptation for site owners to marshal users into tightly controlled pathways, as this enables the site to present its content in what the designers think is the most effective way, whether that be company information, news items or products for sale. At least one site owner has filed a lawsuit to stop other web sites sending visitors to interior pages rather than the homepage. They should be grateful for the traffic, wherever it is directed to.

However, according to a usability study conducted by Jakob Neilson, difficulties in getting from the homepage to the correct product page accounted for 27 per cent of e-commerce failures. A problem, he concludes, that can be in part countered by deep links – those that take the user directly to the right product, without jumping through all of the hoops – in other words, letting the user decide for themselves where they will go.

There are, of course, a couple of provisos. On a large site, it is impossible to link to every article, item, image, product on the site directly from the homepage, or even from secondary information pages. Further, a user should always be given the opportunity to

'escape' back to the homepage or any other page of their choosing from wherever they are on the site (otherwise, they will soon be hitting the back button until they're out of the site, and unlikely to return).

Excessive use of links within blocks of text, too, can cause confusion and irritation as the user quickly forgets where they started on what began as an interesting diversion from the article they were reading, or the product they had selected. To avoid creating forests of text links, the use of icons and images as links, and their prominent positioning on the page, can help attract the user to the most important links (so long as they realise that they are links). Likewise, the proper naming of links is critical – they must tell users in a very economical way where they lead, without deceiving, or again the back button will shortly be in play.

In order to allow users freedom, as a general rule of thumb designers should always link back to the homepage from every page, and possibly include a site search facility. They should always be told where they are, and how to get away – the designer can never know for sure how they got there.

However, while it might be the case that in an ideal world, a user could enter a web site on any page and immediately work out what was going on, in practice the only way this could really happen is on a one page site. Sometimes the designer must force the user to visit one page before another simply so that the second will make sense.

Further, web businesses will inevitably have an interest in getting users to the parts of the site that make money. But rather than forcing users where they don't want to go, attracting them there is always the preferable option. At msn.co.uk, according to Geoff Sutton, 'there is a lot of strategic liaising between the sales team and the network programming team or editorial. It can come in the form of saying that a particular partner company is selling

washing machines, how can we write something entertaining and relevant where a link would be suitable?'

[sputnik7.com] Rolling the cursor over the links on the homepage of this music and video site gives a preview of the most up-to-date content in each section.

DIRECTING INTEREST **STRUCTURE**

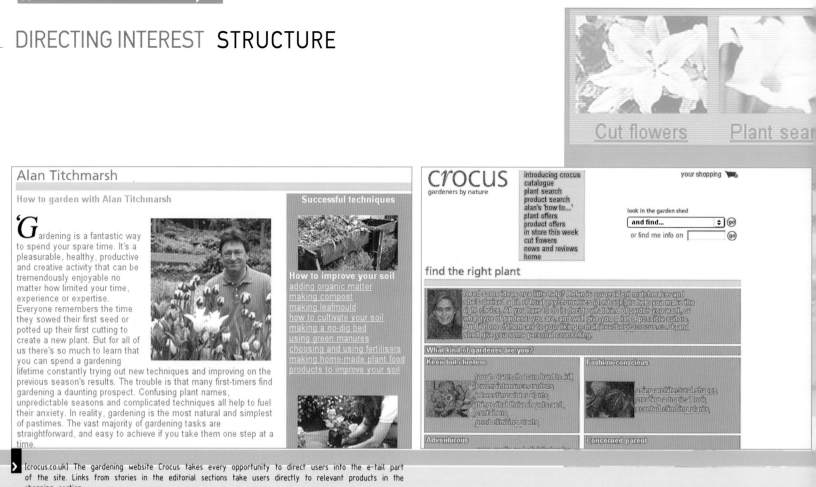

[crocus.co.uk] The gardening website Crocus takes every opportunity to direct users into the e-tail part of the site. Links from stories in the editorial sections take users directly to relevant products in the shopping section.

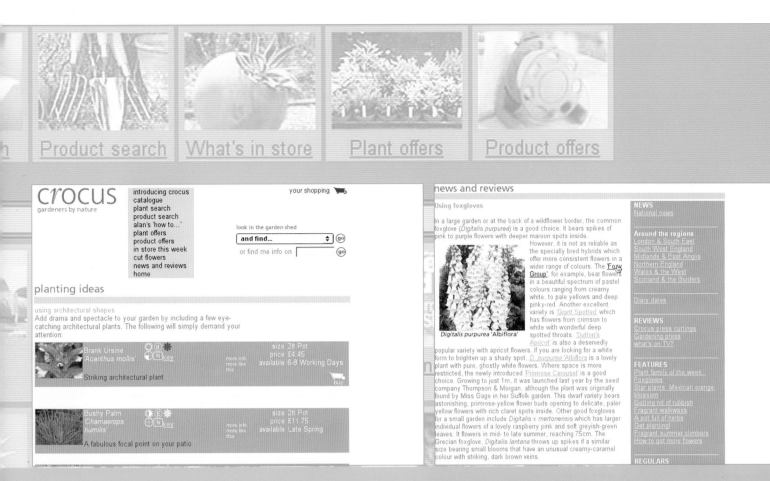

Product search What's in store Plant offers Product offers

crocus
gardeners by nature

introducing crocus
catalogue
plant search
product search
alan's 'how to...'
plant offers
product offers
in store this week
cut flowers
news and reviews
home

your shopping

look in the garden shed

and find... go
or find me info on go

planting ideas

using architectural shapes

Add drama and spectacle to your garden by including a few eye-catching architectural plants. The following will simply demand your attention:

Brank Ursine
'Acanthus mollis'
key

Striking architectural plant

more info
more like this

size 2lt Pot
price £4.45
available 6-8 Working Days

buy

Bushy Palm
Chamaerops humilis'
key

A fabulous focal point on your patio

more info
more like this

size 2lt Pot
price £11.75
available Late Spring

news and reviews

Using foxgloves

In a large garden or at the back of a wildflower border, the common foxglove (*Digitalis purpurea*) is a good choice. It bears spikes of pink to purple flowers with deeper maroon spots inside.

However, it is not as reliable as the specially bred hybrids which offer more consistent flowers in a wider range of colours. The **Foxy Group'**, for example, bear flowers in a beautiful spectrum of pastel colours ranging from creamy white, to pale yellows and deep pinky-red. Another excellent variety is 'Giant Spotted' which has flowers from crimson to white with wonderful deep spotted throats. 'Sutton's Apricot' is also a deservedly popular variety with apricot flowers. If you are looking for a white form to brighten up a shady spot, *D. purpurea 'Albiflora'* is a lovely plant with pure, ghostly white flowers. Where space is more restricted, the newly introduced 'Primrose Carousel' is a good choice. Growing to just 1m, it was launched last year by the seed company Thompson & Morgan, although the plant was originally found by Miss Gage in her Suffolk garden. This dwarf variety bears astonishing, primrose-yellow flower buds opening to delicate, paler yellow flowers with rich claret spots inside. Other good foxgloves for a small garden include *Digitalis x mertonensis* which has larger individual flowers of a lovely raspberry pink and soft greyish-green leaves. It flowers in mid- to late summer, reaching 75cm. The Grecian foxglove, *Digitalis lantana* throws up spikes if a similar size bearing small blooms that have an unusual creamy-caramel colour with striking, dark brown veins.

Digitalis purpurea 'Albiflora'

NEWS
National news

Around the regions
London & South East
South West England
Midlands & East Anglia
Northern England
Wales & the West
Scotland & the Borders

Diary dates

REVIEWS
Crocus press cuttings
Gardening press
What's on TV?

FEATURES
Plant family of the week
Foxgloves
Star plants: Mexican orange blossom
Getting rid of rubbish
Fragrant walkways
A pot full of herbs
Get planting!
Fragrant summer climbers
How to get more flowers

REGULARS

crocus
gardeners by nature

introducing crocus
catalogue
plant search
product search
alan's 'how to...'
plant offers
product offers
in store this week
cut flowers
news and reviews
home

your shopping

look in the garden shed

and find... go
or find me info on go

Foxglove
'Digitalis purpurea Foxy Group'
key

CAUTION: toxic if eaten

Tall spires of tubular flowers in carmine-red, pink, creamy-yellow or white with maroon spotted throats from July to August. These pastel annual foxgloves are considerably shorter than the common native variety. An excellent choice for the back of a partially shady, cottage-style border, they're particularly suitable for exposed, windy sites.

- **Position:** full sun or partial shade
- **Soil:** moist, humus-rich soil
- **Rate of growth:** average to fast-growing
- **Flowering period:** July to August
- **Flower colour:** carmine-red, pink, creamy-yellow or white
- **Other features:** hairy, dark green leaves; all parts of the plant may cause severe discomfort if ingested; contact with the foliage may irritate skin

site map

Apologies for the misnomer, but we thought we'd stick to a term that most people understood. We also reckoned that as long as you could find your way to parts of the site you were interested in, you wouldn't worry what layout or name we used. The only thing that our site map has in common with normal maps is that we have colour coded the main routes around the site. So, the road to shopping is in blue, information in green, and help in purple etc.

Shopping for plants and products

Cut flowers | Plant search | Product search | What's in store | Plant offers | Product offers

Gardening knowhow

Gardening news | Diary dates | What's on tv? | What the papers say | Gardening press | Jobs for the week

Feature of the week | Weather this week | Going organic | Alan's how-to features | Ann-Marie's diary | Star plants

DIRECTING INTEREST **STRUCTURE**

▷ [whatsonwhen.com] As well as using the site as an information resource, users can book flights and hotel accommodation through this international events guide. The opportunity to buy is a constant but unobtrusive presence at the edge of every page.

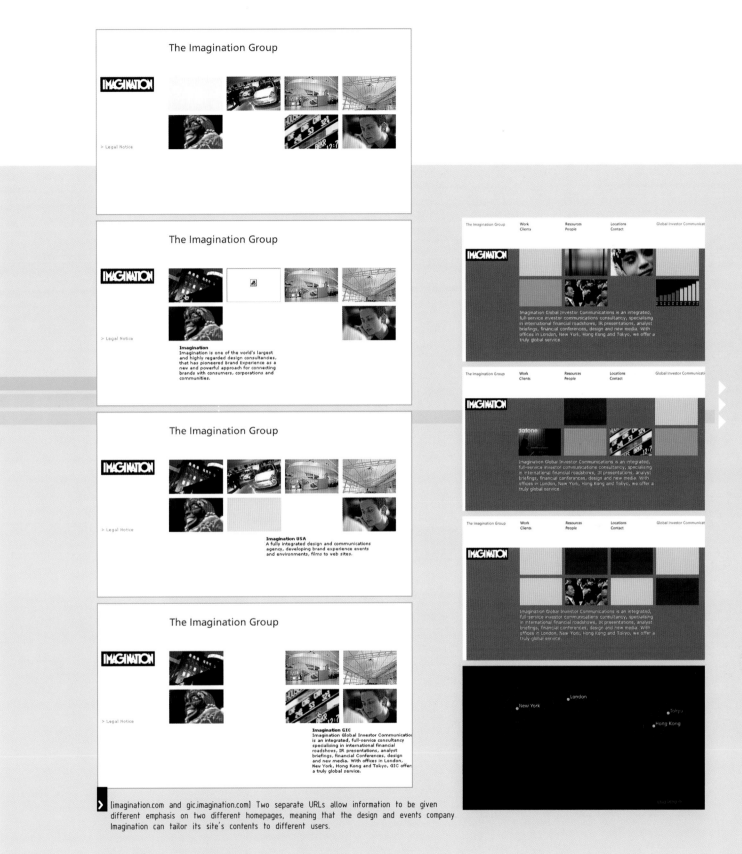

[imagination.com and gic.imagination.com] Two separate URLs allow information to be given different emphasis on two different homepages, meaning that the design and events company Imagination can tailor its site's contents to different users.

DIRECTING INTEREST BUSINESS DEVELOPMENT

The growth and development of business on the web has been marked by two things. One is the number of different business ideas and models – some of which have no equivalent or counterpart in the offline world. The other is that online companies themselves have had to alter their business model as time and market conditions have changed.

Once, first mover advantage was key for some – they had to get a site, any site, online quickly and mark out a territory. For others, they depended solely on advertising to fund their business. However, the online advertising market has changed and it has become apparent that most sites cannot rely on this as a single revenue stream. Naturally, business plans have changed, and the design requirements of sites change with the business plan.

As its site says, reporting the news is just an element of sports.com's business. Offering a range of live scores, contests, fantasy leagues, and electronic merchandise, this fully interactive site keeps sports enthusiasts in touch with their favourite sport. It also sells itself as a 'one stop shop' for companies looking for sports content. This flexibility when it comes to revenue generation has impacted on design requirements, as Damien Meade, head of production at Sports.com observes: 'My brief is basically a rolling brief. The business plan is changing seemingly

every day. So something like gambling has more and more of a presence on the home page of the sports.com site.'

As is often the case, the home page has changed particularly, with an increased emphasis on the most recent news, and in the 'match centres' of the site, which are dedicated to current live games, the offer for people to bet with the site is prominently displayed. 'We have a call to action,' says Damien Meade, 'but we need to strike a balance to give the user an enjoyable experience on the site. We need to tell our users that we need a relationship with them and that they can trust us.'

Fish4, brings together the classified advertising from some 800 newspapers nationwide in the UK but has chosen to focus on the three most popular areas, explains executive producer Douglas McCabe. Its home page presents the three main search sectors of cars, homes and jobs, but does have plenty of white space. 'It should ooze confidence by not trying to sell every piece of real estate on the page,' explains McCabe.

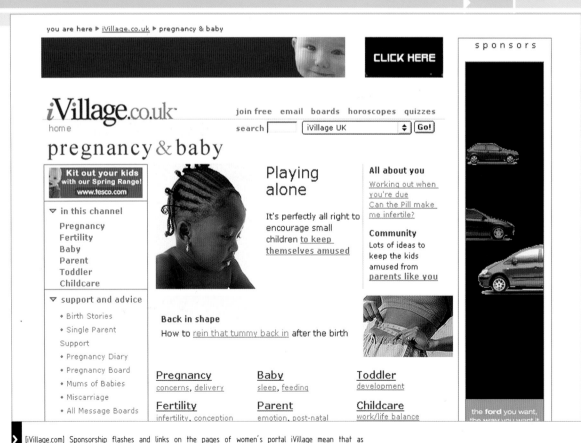

[iVillage.com] Sponsorship flashes and links on the pages of women's portal iVillage mean that as users read about a topic, there are opportunities for them to buy related goods on partner sites – in this case supermarket site tesco.com

> [clickmusic.com] This music site makes a prominent feature of the registration process through pop-ups. The information is useful for profiling users.

> [sports.com] Sports.com is a free content-based site but even in its community sections it provides reminders to users of its other revenue-generating services.

DIRECTING INTEREST AFFILIATES & PARTNERSHIPS

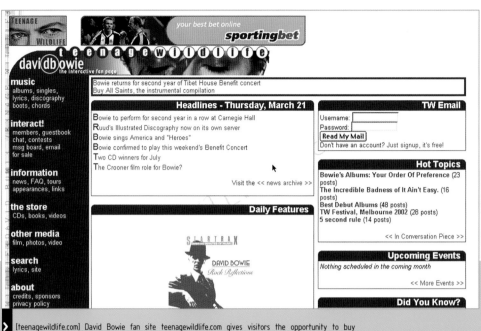

[teenagewildlife.com] David Bowie fan site teenagewildlife.com gives visitors the opportunity to buy Bowie's music at the e-tail site cdnow.com (below). As an affiliate of CDNow, Teenagewildlife will make some commission on any purchase it refers.

There is a way for a site to direct its users to a place where they might spend money, even if the site itself sells nothing: one of the things that sites can do with the people who visit, is guide them on to other web sites. Sure, in its most basic form, this can be done with a simple hypertext link and this is helpful to add context for news stories or promote the site as a resource, or starting point for exploring a particular subject on the web. Or, looking at it the other way, it can be done to give traffic to another site. Of course, if an arrangement is struck where that site offers to pay for each user that visits it via as third-party site, then that can be mutually beneficial. That is basically the concept behind affiliate marketing.

According to Forrester Research, Amazon gets up to 34 per cent of its revenue from its own affiliate programme. It has more than 45,000 members of the network,including many personal sites and small company sites with book review pages, each of whom receives a commission when they redirect a user to Amazon who then completes a purchase. Amazon has the critical mass to set up its own network but a range of third-party affiliate marketing

networks have been set up to promote this idea, such as the American Commission Junction, the British ukaffiliates.com and befree.com.

Like most business ideas online, more and more is being understood about affiliate marketing over time. For one thing, its effectiveness is dictated as much by the quality of the sites and their traffic in the network, not just by how many partners and members there are. Design is one of the criteria which dictates the effectiveness of affiliate sites. For instance, Amazon offers its own specific buttons and banners to its affiliate partners to put them on their sites. Nicky Iapino, UK and Ireland general manager of Commission Junction, which bills itself as a pay-for-performance advertising network, stresses that sites have to meet a set of design criteria before they can join its network. Publishers in the Commission Junction network place ads and links directly in and around content on their web sites. These ads have size guidelines, explains Iapino, which tend to be at the bigger end of the range. 'It's also better for the client site because the advertisers pay

lastminute.com bank holiday 6th May

lastminute.com affiliates programme

Introduction | Agreement | Frequently Asked Questions

Welcome to lastminute.com's Affiliate Programme

Do you run a website and want to earn money from it? Now you are able to link to **lastminute.com** and earn when your visitors buy from our site! It doesn't matter how big or small your site is, you are able to offer your customers the opportunity to buy from a huge range of exciting products and get involved in the e-commerce revolution!

we pay you!

customers visit your website

your site

us!

they then shop at lastminute.com

Apply now!

Want to know more?

- **Earn money.** Sign-up with **lastminute.com** and you can quickly earn money from sales made by visitors to your site - **we pay 2%** (excluding tax) on holiday and hotel transactions.

- **Great products.** Offer a huge range of great value late deals on flights, holidays, hotels, ticket, restaurants and gifts to your visitors.

- **Tips and Support.** We will give you online access to information on promotions, offers, and tips on how to make the most out of the Programme.

- **How do I get paid?** Money is earned from sales generated by your visitors - you can view commission reports at anytime online. You will be paid monthly, if you earn more than £15 - nothing could be simpler!

What do I do next?

1. Look through the Frequently Asked Questions to find out more about the Programme and commissions you can earn.

2. Read the Affiliates Operating Agreement.

3. Complete and submit the online Affiliate Application.

4. We will email you to notify you of the success of your application. You will receive a password and user access to the online reporting site.

5. Use the Affiliate site, http://uk.lastminute.reporting.net to choose banners, links, buttons and products that will appeal to your audience.

6. Visit the Affiliate site, http://uk.lastminute.reporting.net regularly to view reports and read tips to help increase your earnings.

Want to find out more or get in touch? Read the Frequently Asked Questions and if that does not answer your question send an email to affiliates-uk@lastminute.com

Terms & conditions   Apply now!

> [lastminute.com] Sites like lastminute.com, which have successful affilate schemes, dedicate part of their own site to encouraging new partners.

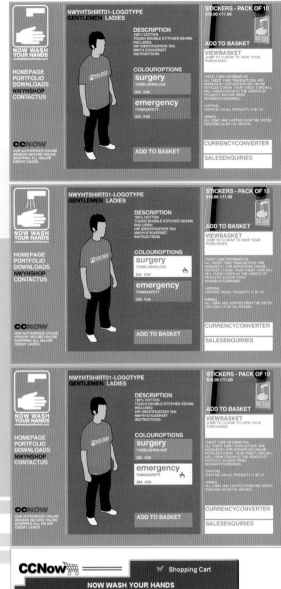

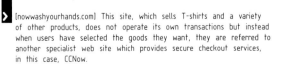

commission rates for traffic and they earn more if they are more successful.' Commission Junction works for a range of sites including offshoots of MSN and Yahoo! and e-tailers like UK catalogue shop Argos. 'We place text links and content links and looking at streaming to make the links more contextual. The key is to be creative and rich with the executions,' she adds.

One creative example Commission Junction brokered for its client handbag.com, a women's portal site, saw links to the retailer mothercare.com on its web site. However, the ads were updated when the content changed to keep them relevant to contemporary content. Effectively, when the page was refreshed, so were the links. Other features included mothercare.com's sponsorship of the 'handbag recommends' links. Iapino concludes: 'If the content on a site changes, you want to change the advertising and the affiliate links to match.'

> [nowwashyourhands.com] This site, which sells T-shirts and a variety of other products, does not operate its own transactions but instead when users have selected the goods they want, they are referred to another specialist web site which provides secure checkout services, in this case, CCNow.

DIRECTING INTEREST AFFILIATES & PARTNERSHIPS

Besides affiliate networks, other relationships are developed between sites, including partnerships. Two key types of partnership can develop online. The first is what we might think of as a true partnership, often based around commissions or a revenue sharing deal of some sort, between two web sites. It often means that one provides the other with the means of offering a relevant service to its users.

For instance, a sports information site could ask a betting site to partner with it so that it can offer its users an opportunity to bet. This is often highlighted with a link and logo on the home page of the host site. This saves it from having to develop its own service, but in the long run it does mean that it is directing traffic away to another site.

The second is for the bigger sites or portals which often have a range of partners who will offer different services to different users. Depending on the market conditions, this dynamic can be the other way. The partner sites want to benefit from the portal's sheer scale of traffic.

The presence and prominence of some partners on a site can change over time. A seasonal business like travel means that certain offers are promoted at different times of the year, says Jon Gisby, head of portals at the UK ISP Freeserve: 'Most of our deals with partners are structured in a way that if there is a good reason why they should be run at a certain time of year it will be.' All such partnersips and affiliate deals, once established, must be constantly reassessed, to keep the site, and the business model, relevant to users.

▷ [timeout.com] Online partners of the magazine and guide Time Out are clearly marked on the relevant pages of the site.

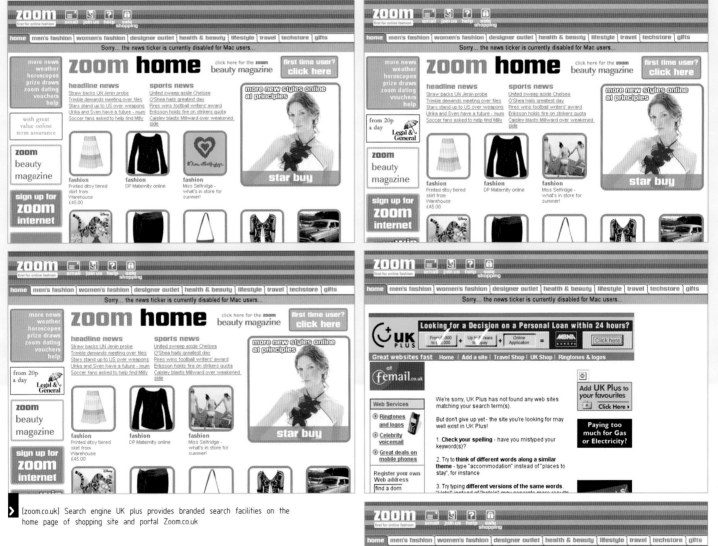

[zoom.co.uk] Search engine UK plus provides branded search facilities on the home page of shopping site and portal Zoom.co.uk

DIRECTING INTEREST PORTALS

In terms of branding, clout and scale, portals tend to be the heavy hitters of the online market. They are among the most visited sites along with major search engines. According to figures from Jupiter MMXI, the Internet research company, MSN, Yahoo!, Lycos, AOL, Tiscali and T-Online, were among the top 10 global domains in Europe in November 2001.

However, 'portals', the catch-all name for these types of sites, can be slightly misleading. They are not all trying to do the same thing or have the same business objective in mind. Although large quanties of traffic are key to their businesses, there are differences. For instance, those that are based in part around offering ISP services, such as the pan-European player Tiscali and the UK's Freeserve, do act as a gateway to the web for some users, hence the portal description. However, as those very same users get more sophisticated, or used to being online, portals try different techniques to be seen as destinations to make money for them and their partners.

This is where smaller sites can learn from them, as they use different strategies to keep users interested in the portal's content and services. MSN's Geoff Sutton says with the range of different services and content on the site – from Hotmail email services to news content – there are two challenges. One is to drive people to the areas which can make more money for MSN; the other is to make more money from the users in the most popular areas. He says that MSN sees itself as more of a network than a portal.

'Our team of editorial people is there to drive people around the site. Links and content are used to interact with the users as much as possible – it is like trying to direct a waterfall. You may want to showcase a health and awareness promotion on a channel on the site but it is fruitless when your users are only going to be interested in a main news event .'

Key to this is the use of what MSN calls a Network Information Pane in the middle of the home page. A series of criteria from relevancy to context and engagement must be met by anything in this area. Sutton explains: 'The idea is that this can be fulfilled by a news story that is breaking or it can be an offer we are running with a diet company at the start of the year when people are looking for these things. It is about finding the right type of content.'

Freeserve's home page serves three different and distinctive roles for the ISP and portal, explains Jon Gisby, head of portals at Freeserve. 'New users want to know about the ISP business. Our commercial partners are represented in a mix of media from special banners to pop-ups and formats like dropdown ads. And there are our tenancy partners who have paid for exposure and sometimes guaranteed levels of traffic.' He adds: 'We have to be flexible to be news-led. The point is that the parts that people want are not necessarily the ones that make the most money.'

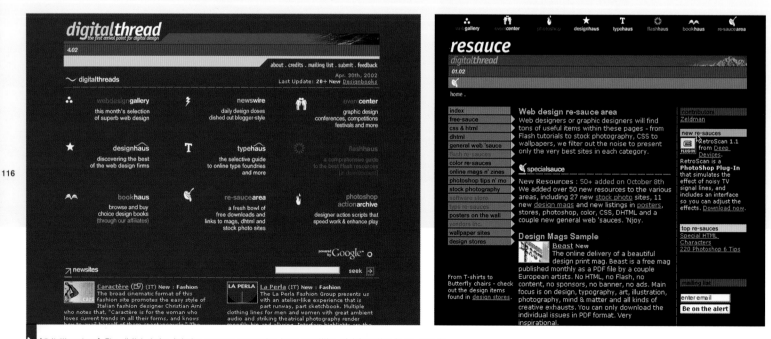

[digitalthread.com] The digital design industry resource aggregates large quantities of information in an easy to navigate format.

[freeserve.co.uk] The ISP's homepage does not force users into the areas of the site that make money, but makes the links obvious.

[msn.co.uk] MSN's Network Information Pane is prominently displayed, and brings together lead features from different parts of the site.

degriftour.com
lastminute.com

eBAY — c'est d'abord sur eBay !
cliquez ici

L'engagement de confiance ☎ 0892 23 01 01 0.34 €/min

accueil | vols | voyages | hôtels | restaurants | cadeaux | adrénaline | sorties | aide / infos +

Loisirs

Pilotage avion (proche Paris)
Prenez les commandes d'un appareil puissant et racé.
Une expérience unique !

L'Epopée du buveur d'eau
Comédie à découvrir absolument !
Commandez une place, nous vous en réservons deux !

Survol en hélicoptère (proche Paris)
Découvrez les châteaux de la Vallée de Chevreuse
Une occasion à ne pas manquer !

CUP OF TEA

Affiliation !
Devenez partenaire de lastminute.com / degriftour.com

lastminute.com

Voyages — Vols — Spécial France — Hôtels — Locations

Restaurants — Sorties — Location de Voitures — Adrénaline — Cadeaux

nos meilleures offres !

Nouveau service : Réservez votre billet de train en ligne.

Recevez tous nos bons plans !   >>e-mail< Ok !

recherchez parmi nos 12 300 offres voyages*

○ séjours à l'étranger   ○ séjours en France   ○ billets d'avion

Destination:
Choix de la destination ▼

Votre ville de départ:
Indifférent ▼

Votre date de départ:
[   ] 📅 ± 4 ▲▼ jours
JJ/MM/AA

Le prix de vos vacances:
Tous les prix ▼

Durée du séjour:
Toutes les durées ▼

Séjour à thème:
Toutes nos suggestions ▼

Formule de vacances:
Toutes les formules ▼

▶ partez !

*dernière mise à jour du catalogue samedi 27 avril, 17:10

Ponts de mai
🗺 cliquez ici

Dernière minute !

Bretagne - Résidence Thalassa la Falaise 3*
La Mer, la Santé et beaucoup de Bien Etre à Dinard !
Réduction jusqu'à 40 %

Italie - 4 nuits dont 2 à Florence
A partir de 280 €

Istanbul
Court séjour pont de mai ! 4 nuits en hôtel 3*
A partir de 199 €

Tunisie
Hôtel club " les pieds dans l'eau ! " en pension complète
Plus de 30 % de réduction

Les Jardins de Paris, 8 hôtels à découvrir !
Jusqu'à 40 % de réduction

avec Thai Airways

à saisir !

▶ Week-end du 1er Mai en Tunisie Départ le 01/05 A partir de 420,00 € TTC (2 755,02 FRF TTC)

▶ St Raphael 2 pièces 3-4 personnes à partir du

↓   → Degriftour homepage.

↓

degriftour.com
lastminute.com

eBAY — neuf ou occasion, les grandes marques Pentium III
cliquez ici

L'engagement de confiance ☎ 0892 23 01 01 0.34 €/min

accueil | vols | voyages | hôtels | restaurants | cadeaux | adrénaline | sorties | aide / infos +

RECHERCHE PAR CRITERES

Entrez vos critères...

Toutes les destinations ▼

Toutes les dates ▼

Toutes les villes de départ ▼

Toutes nos suggestions ▼

Tous les prix ▼

...puis consultez **toutes nos bonnes affaires**

▶ j'y vais !

Vols (9104 offres)

NOS BONNES AFFAIRES
...consultez tout notre catalogue :

[9027 offres]   [77 offres]

Vols Charters / Reguliers   Vols Affaires

L'ENSEMBLE DES OFFRES DU MARCHE
...recherchez par notre puissant moteur:

Vous partez de:
[   ]

Date de départ:
[   ] 📅
Ex. : 01/11/00, 02/04/2000...

Vous allez à:
[   ]

Date de retour:
[   ] 📅
Ex. : 01/11/00, 02/04/2000...

Nb d'adultes:
1 ▼

Enfant:
0 ▼
(2 à 11 ans)

Bébé:
0 ▼
(0 à 2 ans)

▶ rechercher

→ Degriftour search facility.

Degriftour

→ Lastminute.com homepage.

French online travel site Degriftour is the result of two big online brands coming together. In August 2000, the UK dotcom lastminute.com announced that it was buying the Degriftour Group to gain its 250,000 customers, an inventory from its French suppliers and a further foothold in the French market.

However, in the time since, the new company has had to pull off a delicate balancing act in order to pull the Degriftour site into the lastminute.com network without offending or alienating its existing customers. Its web site reflects that balancing act.

According to Chris Cleave, head of customer experience at lastminute.com, the trick was to preserve the value of the Degriftour brand and client base and lever lastminute.com technology into its business to give it global distribution possibilities.

This means that the French site is different from the rest of the lastminute.com network of country sites. 'It is gradually evolving to look like the global solution,' Cleave says. 'It all happened at the user interface level. There was no hurry and no extra cost to have two separate user interfaces in the same country.' He adds: 'Initially we started off by adding extra stuff to the Degriftour site in terms of product categories. It only offered travel and we added Theatre and Adrenalin and Restaurants.' Then it was the turn of the navigation bar which was changed on both the French lastminute site and Degriftour's site to eventually make them look different, but similar to each other. Elements of each brand's colour were added to both sites – lastminute.com's pink and Degriftour's blue. One thing that changed immediately was the addition of the lastminute.com name to Degriftour's home page. Over time that name and logo has become bigger.

119

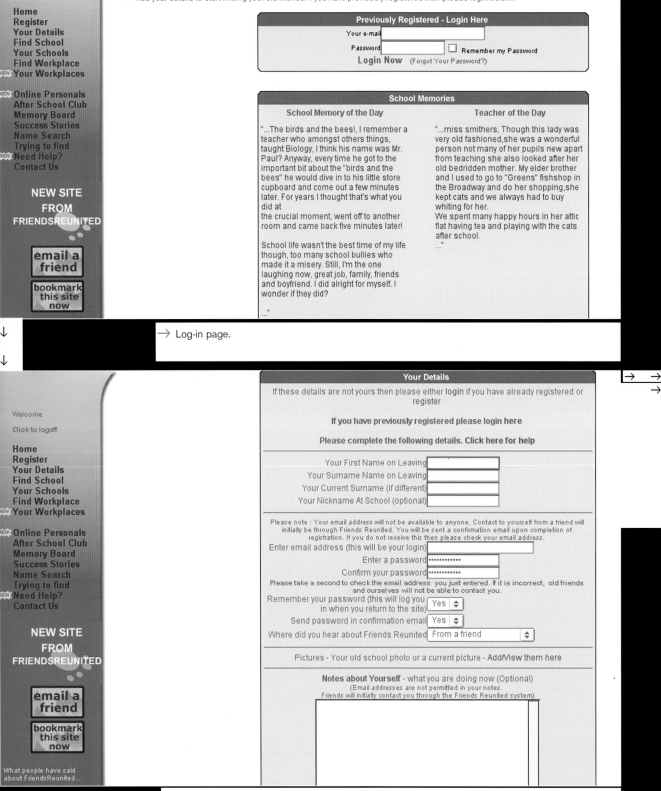

→ Log-in page.

→ Registration page.

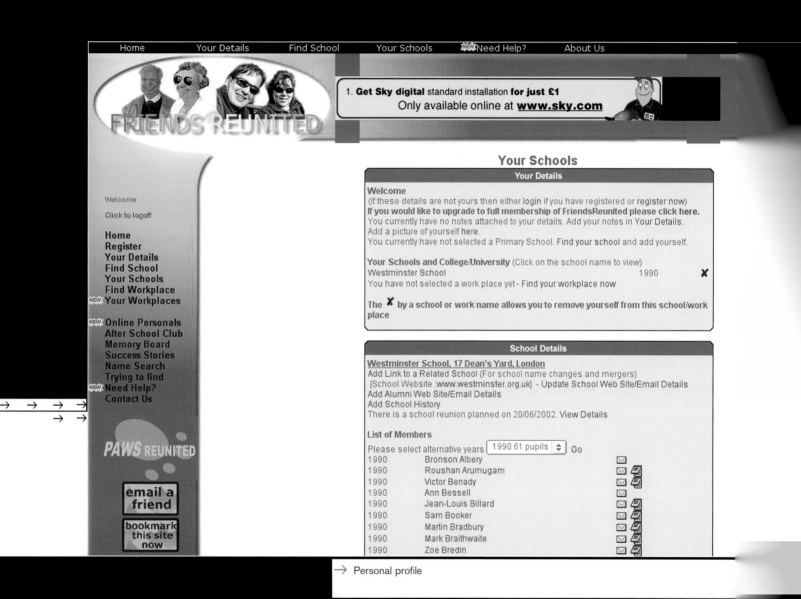

→ Personal profile

If one site has illustrated that a simple idea and straightforward execution can succeed in capturing the imagination of millions, while vast sums of Venture Capital cash can be spent on an online business with little return, it is Friends Reunited, the site that allows old school friends to regain contact with one another. From its humble beginnings in the upstairs room of a house in Barnet, North London, where it was started by husband and wife team Steve and Julie Pankhurst, Friends Reunited has become one of the most visited sites in the UK in little more than a year. According to Nielsen//NetRatings, by October 2001 it had almost 1.5million unique visitors at home. At that stage its database has registered some 40,000 Secondary and Primary Schools, Colleges and Universities in Britain. More than 2.5 million people have registered and this is growing at over 20,000 a day.

Yet the design of the site remains as 'unsophisticated' as ever. Steve Pankhurst, co-founder of Friends Reunited, however, delights in its so-called amateurish feel. 'A lot of our users are new to the Internet,' he explains. 'The key is to make it simple. There is one old couple who apparently think that the Internet is just Friends Reunited – so we have been careful to not put too much in that they would not

→ School search.

CASE STUDY

→ Friends Reuni

→ Members' profiles.

not understand.' Effectively, he says the design is almost an anti-design. As a software and database specialist, he says it is all about making the database as accessible as possible to the users. 'It wasn't about the design when we launched – it was about making it as easy as possible to get to the database of schools and the former pupils. We wrote our own systems with no frills and as few clicks as possible.' This has obviously aided the site's growth and popularity. According to Nielsen//NetRatings' analysis in June 2001, the site was getting some 20 per cent of its visitors from web-based email sites which implies a word-of-mouth viral marketing element in its success. Pankhurst sums it up: 'The whole point is that the design should not get in the way of what the site should do. The graphics are grainy and a time may come when we may change it. But if it is not broken then why should we fix it?'

RESPONDING WITH INTEREST

Figleaves Voucher :

Collect your **FREE** £5 voucher here!

Figleaves.com carries all the names that matter in the world of underwear. With over 70 men's and women's brands to choose from you're sure to find something that suits your style. What's more, with our fast free delivery service and no quibbles, free return policy, you'll never be stuck with something that you don't like.

Enter your email address here to receive a FREE £5 voucher:

SEND ME THE VOUCHER

£5

The offer applies to a minimum spend of £15 and only one voucher per person is available. Terms and conditions for voucher usage are included on the email you will receive.

If you have any problems either email the customer services team or call our customer helpdesk on **020 8492 1300**

Great selection
- Big Name Brands
- Designer Fashions
- Men's Brands
- Swimwear

Lejaby - Intention underwired full cup bra **£37.00**

Gossard - Ultrabra Airotic bra **£28.00**

Ben Sherman - Woven Cotton boxer short **£13.00**

Footprints - Onyx soft cup swimsuit **£39.00**

BRAS FINDER™   BRIEFS FINDER™   LEGS FINDER™   BEST SELLERS   FEEDBACK

▷ [figleaves.com] Online lingerie retailer figleaves.com uses sales promotions and loyalty schemes to incentivise users to return to the site.

mykindaplace.com — zed's new**SMS Chat** zed

home   showbiz music   chill in   film life cringe fashion beauty   work it   agony shop fun mobile chat stars

Member login
Username   Password

Join MKP ⇨

WIN

search the web

click to win
- fortune dragon
- mykindachat
- make MKP my homepage
- sign up for newsletter
- get your racing frog
- celeb voicemails

▌▌ **Free Membership**

Register for free and receive your exclusive personal futurology reading as a special welcome treat. mykindaplace.com members can enter our fab competitions, chat in one of our cool chat rooms AND receive our weekly newsletter to keep you up-to-date with all the latest showbiz news, reviews, interviews and much, much more!

▌▌ **Your Details**

First name   Last name
Username   Password (5-10 characters)
(only use letters and numbers, 1-15 characters)   Confirm Password

Sex   ◉ Babe ○ Boy   Date of birth MM ▢ DD ▢ 19
Remember my login ☐ Help
Email address   Mobile number 07
(UK only. numbers must begin with 07)

Password reminder phrase   What's your mother's maiden name? ▢
Password reminder phrase answer

▌▌ **Your Address**

If you enter competitions and win you'll need to give us your address so we can send you your prize. Don't miss out!

Address line 1   Address line 2
Town/County   Postcode
Country United Kingdom ▢

*Optional *Essential for futurology reading

next page ▌▌▷

▷ [mykindaplace.com] Of course the easiest way to get details of your users is to ask them for them which you can use to stay in contact. However, some users can be put off by questions they deem too personal or by the perceived 'hassle' of filling in long forms. Many sites persuade users to give basic information through membership registration, which allows them access to parts of the site that would otherwise be closed to them.

126

A lot of effort goes into attracting new users to a site and encouraging them to explore when they get there. Hopefully, they enjoy the experience and will wish to return. But it is one thing to want the user to come back to the site, and another, in a multi-channelled world, to remind them effectively. Unless the web site is the offshoot of an established offline business, people are not reminded of its existence when they go to the shopping mall, or the local high street or go about their day-to-day business offline.

Naturally, when a user visits a site, there is an opportunity to gather information which can be used to develop the relationship. But it is difficult for a user to immediately trust a site, particularly if it is new or is still developing its brand, with all of his or her details. Most people, however, are happy to give their name and email address. Usually only after being incentivised, for example with the opportunity to win things, do they give up more specific and personal details.

With the use of cookies, the technology which gives access to a user's individual computer, this process can be speeded up. For instance shoppers on Amazon.com with a cookie from the site on their PC will be welcomed by name. They can even ask for recommendations based on a purchase history. Most e-tailers base their recommendations on the idea that if a user buys a certain product, they might be interested in the products that other people who have it, bought at the same time. So-called personalisation like this works by treating people who are interested in music by a certain soul singer, say, as a group, not by treating each and every person as an individual and it should not claim to do so. Nevertheless, it is in itself a helpful service and gives users the perception that their needs are considered by the site. Personalisation on this scale requires some sophisticated software, but similar effects can be achieved more easily, through allowing users to set background colour preferences, for example, or by making use of the personal nature of email.

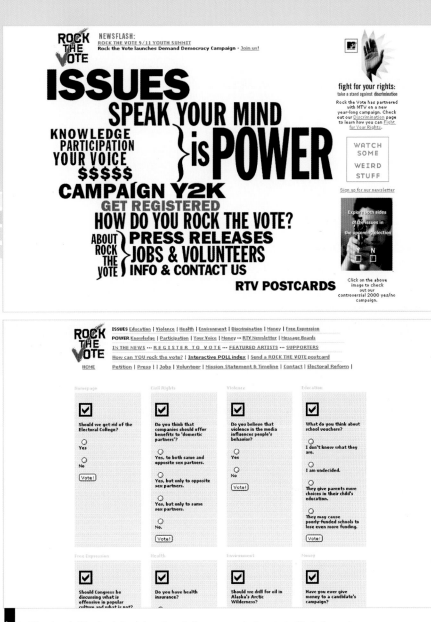

> [rockthevote.org] This site designed to get apathetic young people to vote in US elections gets them in the mood for democracy by taking polls on the site. Polls and surveys can be a useful way of giving users a feeling of belonging to the site.

127

or by making use of the personal nature of email.
For instance, an international record company like BMG will
contact the fans of existing bands on its roster by email when it
is about to launch a similar pop act to one a user of its sites has
previously expressed an interest in. It is also keen to build up
existing relationships through a wide range of different digital
channels. Fans of the Irish boyband Westlife can contact the band
through its web site via email but can also get a text message to
their mobile phones every two weeks. Teenagers are far happier
than most to interact via SMS.

Sites need to interact with users often enough to stay in touch,
but must avoid appearing intrusive. An email or text message
which is inappropriate or unwanted can be more annoying than
standard junk mail offline due to the more highly personal nature
of the technology.

Marketeers and web site owners should appreciate this but
also realise the potential for interacting with and developing
relationships with consumers and users in exciting and
different ways.

[abctales.com] The writers' site ABCTales requires users to register in
order to access content.

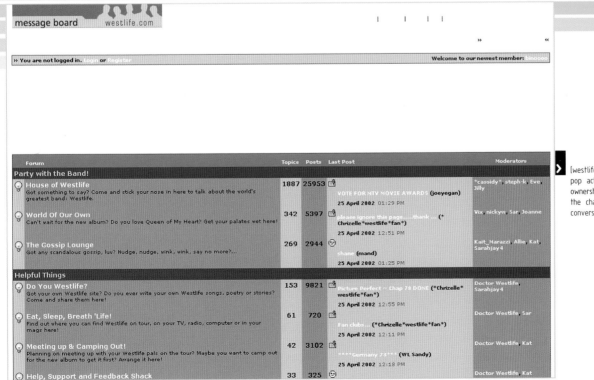

[silicon.com] Users of the IT news site silicon.com can interact with it in several ways. Readers can email the journalists and authors of each story and they are able to personalise the site so that they see the stories on areas that might particularly interest them when they return.

[westlife.co.uk] Bulletin boards, such as this for teen pop act Westlife, encourage a sense of community and ownership of the site by its users, thereby increasing the chances that they will return to the site as conversations and messages develop.

129

RESPONDING WITH INTEREST **POLLS & SURVEYS**

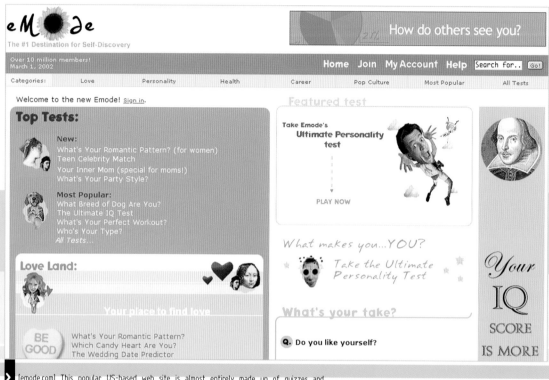

> [emode.com] This popular US-based web site is almost entirely made up of quizzes and questionnaires covering every aspect of personality and lifestyle, demonstrating the extent to which users enjoy interacting with sites when the content is presented in the right way.

Polls and surveys asking what users think of the site are not only useful for creating 'relationships' with users, but also allow the site owner to tweak the design and content to maximise user satisfaction This can be used in conjunction with the digital tracking of users' movements around the site to assess what is and isn't working.

It is one thing to monitor what the user is doing on your web site, particularly if it is an e-commerce web site where the success or otherwise of the shopping experience is easily measured. For instance, if a potential shopper has left the site after choosing some items and beginning the actual buying process the reasons behind their decision can be narrowed down.

However, for other sites not only can the success or otherwise of the site in the eyes of the user be hard to anticipate, but also any aspirations that the user may have for the site be untapped. Particularly, if the site in question is run by a publisher trading on the quality of content and what it can add and offer to the brand.

One answer can be to actually ask the user by presenting them with an online questionnaire. This needs to be handled carefully as, if presented in the wrong way, it can be seen as intrusive.

'A few years back most web sites were developed without knowing what their visitors want and what they wanted to do. It now makes sense to do that,' says Kjell Oksendal, marketing

manager of Firm, which provides a range of sites, from Virgin.net to FT.com to Yell.com, with the software to survey their users. 'Media owners and corporate sites do not necessarily conduct an online sales process – they are used for information. These sites can have huge numbers of visitors but not the ones who will often make email requests or telephone contact. So when they register for something or stop and are about to leave the site – why not ask them why?'

This is usually in the form of a pop-up, which should not slow a user in a hurry as they can opt out of answering by closing it. Portals can benefit in particular, he claims. 'It helps them to get a cross section of the broad range of users on any one site, because they have an audience that wants to fulfil many needs.'

There are other alternatives to offering the questionnaire. 'If the site is only accessed by registered users then the survey can be conducted by email,' Oksendal suggests. 'You can incentivise users to answer but give them a unique URL each time so that they answer only once.' Frequency can be capped as well so that say one in every 10 users is questioned.

Running polls and surveys on general issues, not related to the performance of the site, can also be a very useful way of allowing users to interact with the site, and feel that they have a stake in its content. In this context, the poll forms part of the entertainment provided by the site.

[extraordinaryworld.com] Famously opinionated football fans are given a number of opportunities to share their views on this UK-based site: they can vote in viewers' polls, contribute to a discussion forum, or rate the site itself in a league run by football portal alphasoccer (below), thus drawing attention and more traffic to the extraordinary world.

RESPONDING WITH INTEREST POLLS & SURVEYS

[bbc.co.uk] Users of the BBC's news site can contribute to Talking Points pages, where major news events are discussed.

[trailervision.com] The trailers for imaginary films on the Trailervision web site are rated by the users and form their own list of top trailers. Allowing fans to rate content in this way should ensure that not only do they feel involved with the site, but that the elements of the site most likely to appeal to other visitors are brought to their attention.

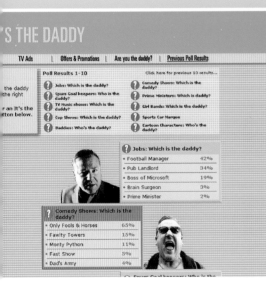

133

[itsthedaddy.com] Beer brand Holsten pils claimed in its offline advertising to be 'the daddy' of all drinks. A web site was designed to support the campaign by asking users to vote for the 'daddy' in a wide variety of fields, ranging from fictional detectives and take-away foods to famous men called Frank. The polls changed every day, encouraging users to return regularly.

RESPONDING WITH INTEREST COMMUNITIES

One of the initial mantras for running businesses in the new economy was that the most successful sites revolved around the three 'C's' of content, commerce and community. It should not be dismissed out of hand as an idea – some successful sites do offer an element of all three, though very few place equal emphasis on each of the elements. Fewer still do that to the exclusion of other assets and attributes.

However, looked at in a certain light, even a successful e-tailer like Amazon does have all three elements. It has commerce, obviously. It has content in the form of book reviews and previews and features on writers and musicians, and a limited form of community in that users post their own reviews on the site.

However, it is not a true community. A true community, as Felix Velarde of digital agency Underwired* explains, is when users communicate directly with each other. This can become an attraction in its own right as viewing conversations or threads and postings to see what the latest topic is can be as engaging as actually taking part.

Communities can build up around all sorts of enthusiasms and topics, from doll collectors to sufferers of a particular illness. The main design imperative on these sorts of community sections is to allow the conversation to flow, so speed of response is more

important than anything else. Postings are accompanied by a user name or nickname, date, time and subject lines and little else, apart from the occasional use of icons to highlight the latest or most abusive (flame) posts.

More recently, the concept of a community as an entity that exists both on- and offline has been developed. The UK-based site beyondbricks.com is designed to encourage new media entrepreneurs to talk online and offers experts for them to talk to. But it is designed to operate as an offline community as well and the BB organisation, which is backed by the government's Department of Trade and Industry, runs a series of networking events, which promote the web site beyondbricks.com.

[habbohotel.com] Visitors to this community site are represented by 3-D avatars which travel around a virtual world.

profile   inbox   register   calendar   members   faq   search   home   logout

IRON MAIDEN
OFFICIAL WEBSITE

Earboards.com > Band Forums > Iron Maiden

Forum	Posts	Threads	Last Post	Moderator
On Topic				
Maiden-related Talk				
General Music Discussion For musical discussion. Please use the Chat forum for off-topic talk.	10179	839	03-01-2002 03:20 PM by sostos	Lord SUMMERISLE, Mark, Ruined Luna
Musicians Discussion	113	18	03-01-2002 03:09 PM by Gonzo	Mark
Band Members Forums for each member, as well as one for Ex-Members.	247	26	03-01-2002 01:26 PM by the_trooper@maiden4ever	
Ex-Members What are they up to?	83	9	03-01-2002 09:44 AM by Uncletrunx	Mark, Ruined Luna
Clive Burr Support	366	284	03-01-2002 12:17 PM by GhostofCain	Mark
Brixton Gig Discussion Arrange meet-ups here!	1524	217	03-01-2002 03:01 PM by Kelly	Mark
Off-Topic				
Chat General non-music discussion in here	13466	878	03-01-2002 03:20 PM by JimD	ALF, Lord SUMMERISLE, Mark, Ruined Luna, shrike
Utter Nonsense Go crazy!	6776	144	03-01-2002 03:04 PM by Kelly	ALF, Lord SUMMERISLE
Trade	1930	424	02-28-2002 10:00 PM by tk2709	
Alt.Lyrics Rewrite the lyrics to your fave Maiden track	4493	885	02-28-2002 11:07 PM by Uncletrunx	
Admin				
Announcements	36	33	02-18-2002 05:14 PM by Skunk	
Addie's Challenge	3382	286	02-12-2002 09:19 PM by Ashwin_reddy	
Chatroom Help For forum help, please visit the forums in Forum Control	37	9	03-01-2002 02:54 AM by McBrain's Brain	

> [ironmaiden.com] Fans of the heavy metal band Iron Maiden can use icons to express their emotions and moods on its message board.

T Threadless.com. Stop The Nudity.   view cart. account. join. log in

shop > product catalog. specials. stock chart   participate > score submissions. forum. submit

Threadless shopping. our newest product arrivals   Threadless design competitions

Design, Submit, Score, Judge
72 submissions in the running

Accepting Applications
We will choose 12 designers over the summer to design for each month of the calendar

Accepting Applications
Poster designers will be chosen at random times from the application list

Threadless forum activity

General Discussion	Today
Submission Gossip	Today
Site Feedback	04/20/02
Threadless Posters	04/08/02
Threadless Clothing	04/24/02

Three random submissions in the running

T **Threadless.com. Stop The Nudity.**   view cart. account. join. log in

shop > product catalog. specials. stock chart   participate > score submissions. forum. submit

Discussion forum

threadless forums > General Discussion

Band Shirts

To post, login.

fine-point on 03/14/02 · 4:39 PM   e-mail | profile | edit

I keep seeing submissions with bands names on them. What do you guys think of these?

I think they generally look good...but I dont understand why you would submit them. I know its because you are a fan of the band...so then why not send it to the band? If they like it and use it youre bound to get the same things your get from Threadless (free shirts, credit, bragging rights etc). Plus (I said it before...ill say it again) youd be helping this band make money. Bands like that get paid shit by venues and merch is how they survive. If your submission was to win, you might be helping them in the free advertising dept, but you could also be hurting them in terms of sales.

Just a thought. This in no way is targeted at Threadless or a certain Tee or Designer (hence the General Discussion topic)...so please dont take it that way. Its also not meant to be taken as bitchy or pissed. Just a conversation starter. Im really interested in hearing your thoughts and points, agreeing and counter alike.

alexhindle on 03/14/02 · 5:44 PM   e-mail | profile | edit

damn right

jooser on 03/14/02 · 6:09 PM   e-mail | profile | edit

i tend to agree. this is a place for ORIGINAL design ideas, band t-shirts are all well and good (christ knows theres enough bad ones) but i'd rather see something i wouldn't see anywhere else. cool & quirky illustrations or icons are the best - ctrl+ z, halfproject, he-shoot etc.

hugbot on 03/14/02 · 8:41 PM   edit

yeah, well, that's what i feel about having web addresses on shirts. if someone made a t-shirt with my band name on it, i'd think it was sort of cool, but if i knew that they'd used someone else to produce it (i.e. threadless) who had no interest in my band, i'd feel cheated and pissed.

suburban on 03/14/02 · 9:30 PM   e-mail | profile | edit

Yes and wouldn't we all Hugbot...wouldn't we all.

> [threadless.com] Unusually for an e-tailer, t-shirt producer Threadless.com has built a community of its customers and designers.

135

RESPONDING WITH INTEREST LOYALTY

During the 90s, the concept of loyalty schemes in the offline world expanded and proliferated as never before. From supermarket chains offering incentive points for each purchase to airlines offering free travel with each mile flown by a customer, the concept became instinctive and helped the notion gain currency.

The idea has also lent itself to the online world. If a shopper earns more for their money in the form of money-off or a free product or service, they are more likely to return and develop loyalty to the site. Not only did sites develop their own reward schemes, but specific schemes such as Beenz and web rewards became brands in their own right and partnered with a network of sites that could offer and redeem their units. Before its demise in 2001, Beenz even billed itself as an online currency with its ambition to become a global brand.

US-based reward scheme MyPoints offers money off from sites like Barnes & Noble and Blockbuster Video. It gives MyPoints for a range of activities from just visiting some sites to using email as well as buying goods through MyPoints Shopping. Sites where points can be redeemed set up branded pages off their homepage

to welcome users – members of a particular scheme will have to highlight their participation by placing a logo in a prominent position.

Likewise, lingerie etailer Figleaves is a member of the ipoints scheme and has a logo on the righthand side of its homepage next to other badges of certification. Accessing a link on the ipoints site brings the user to a branded part of the Figleaves.com site which allows users to fill in an email address to get a £10 voucher to spend on the lingerie site.

136

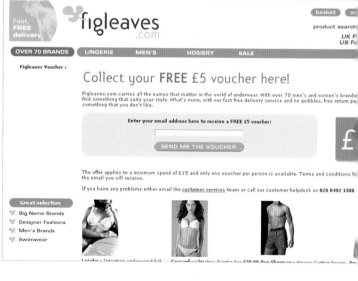

[figleaves.com] Retailer figleaves.com has a dedicated section of its site for the redemption of points from third party reward schemes.

[toptable.co.uk] Restaurant booking and reservation site toptable.co.uk is a partner in the Internet reward scheme ipoints. Users earn units when they buy products and services from the scheme's partners, which can then be spent on more goods and services from participating sites.

RESPONDING WITH INTEREST PERSONALISATION

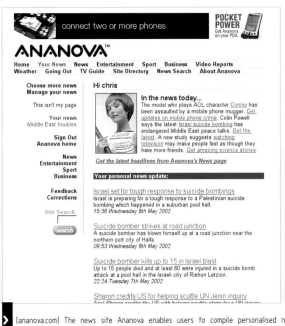

[ananova.com] The news site Ananova enables users to compile personalised news by selecting topics likely to interest them.

[floodgear.com] The designer's web site Flood Gear asks users to 'personalise' it by choosing emotions according to their mood when they visit the web site, and adding their feelings to other users' in a list. Although this is not true personalisation, it has a similar effect as users are able to see their words reproduced on the site.

NEWS DOWNLOADS KISSES

PORTFOLIO

WALLPAPERS

AUTHOR

LINKS

KISSES
how do you feel?   (because...)
good   I'm being productive   FLOOD

LUNCH BREAK
SANTA MONICA BEACH

KISS ME   INTIMATE STRANGER

FLOOD GEAR
STIMULATE YOUR D:BODY

ART|EYE
PARTNER SITE

Web users are individuals with different interests and tastes – and want to be treated as such. So whether they are shoppers or readers of online information, their individual preferences should be catered for as far as possible.

Personalisation means that the user gets bespoke content or services that are tailored to their tastes, which can be measured in a variety of ways. They can opt-in and state preferences, or choices and offers can be made on the basis of users' past actions and behaviour.

Ananova, the consumer-facing news site, has a homepage designed with personalisation in mind. A wide range of news stories is offered, and readers are able to tick boxes to collate stories of the type that interest them most. It calls the service Your News. The site offers additional personalisation in that 'your news' can be emailed to individual users, who can also post their own news profiles on the site for the interest of other readers.

Some sites allow users to adjust the appearance of the content to suit their tastes, but not select the content itself. MSN, for example, lets the user alter the design through My MSN, but does not surrender absolute control. After all, it is a business, so although the user can prioritise what they see first in terms of content and services, MSN still wishes to offer promotions to all users, for example. 'We are slightly schizophrenic about this,' admits Geoff Sutton, director of MSN UK, 'in that it is important for us to be able to promote the right things at the right time to the right people. Also, even if you choose everything you want specifically, you can still be missing out on content that you might be interested in. I may choose to see the results of my favourite football team but I might still be interested in a cheap holiday offer.'

NEWS DOWNLOADS KISSES

KISSES

PORTFOLIO

WALLPAPERS

AUTHOR

LINKS

good. I'm being productive
rejected. mothing
lucky. I found you
pissed off. php refuses to install with apache
lucky.
orange.
drunk. I've drunk
sleepy.
useless. I'm not appreciated
sleepy.
confused. i dont know what this thing is!
speechless.
useless. I am
ok.
pissed off. i'm must build a complete website in 4 hours
ecstatic!. tjas
speechless.
homy. luke is my man
speechless. 5445
pissed off. of my mum

o is you

FLOOD GEAR
STIMULATE YOUR D:BODY

ART|EYE
PARTNER SITE

139

RESPONDING WITH INTEREST PERSONALISATION

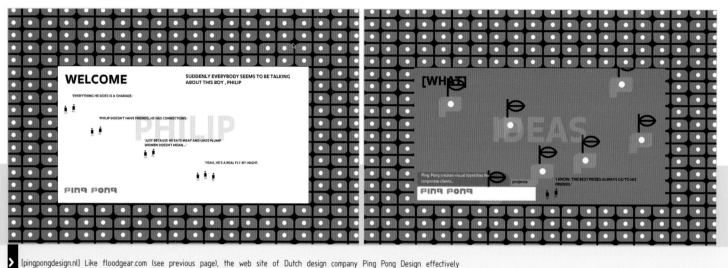

▶ [pingpongdesign.nl] Like floodgear.com (see previous page), the web site of Dutch design company Ping Pong Design effectively simulates personalisation by asking users to type in their name when they arrive. Animated messages then start to recount the nice things that everybody is apparently saying about them.

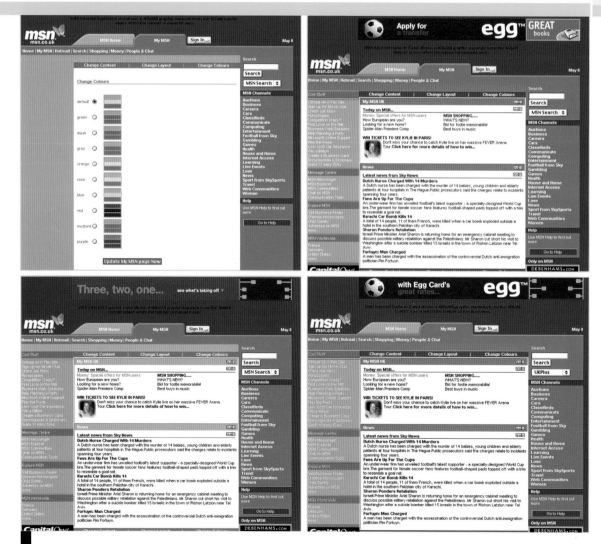

▶ [msn.co.uk] Although MSN retains ultimate control over what content is displayed, it allows users to choose a layout and colour scheme, and set preferences for news and information.

Freeserve, the UK ISP, has taken the opposite view. It did offer personalisation once but has given up. According to Jon Gisby, head of portals at Freeserve, it can work but is hard to get right. 'We don't have it at the moment. In our experience it is hard to implement and most of users see it as being about the tools themselves, not the services and the content. It is less of a concern at the moment.'

Amazon is noted for its personalisation, and other etailers place a priority on it. Not only should it bring users back to a site but it is also thought to help convert them from browsers to active shoppers with tailored promotions.

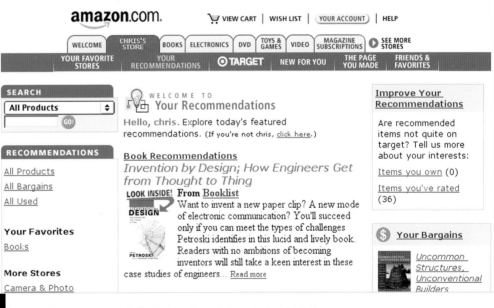

[amazon.com] Amazon uses personalisation to get customers to buy again from its site by 'recommending' books or music according to their registered tastes. Once users have enjoyed this feature, they will often return to the site just to see what recommendations have been made.

RESPONDING WITH INTEREST EMAIL ALERTS

If a business is trying to coax users back to a web site then it makes sense for it to use other digital channels. And a lot of the same principles for the use of email and SMS messages as when trying to attract users in the first place (see chapter one) still apply. A significant difference is that the site can exploit knowledge of the users' habits to make the communication more relevant.

This is important. As lastminute.com's Chris Cleave explains, for an e-tailer, retaining customers is the hardest thing to do on the Internet because they simply have so much choice online. As well as endeavouring to ensure that a shopper's experience with a site is perfect the first and every time – which is as difficult to do as it sounds – lastminute.com concentrates on direct marketing. 'It makes sense for an email to greet people who have booked a holiday through our site when they return asking "How was it?"' says Cleave. 'And they can be contacted again a year later and the odds are they might want another holiday.'

The US-based lifestyle site Emode regularly sends users questionnaires via email offering to tell them more about their personality and lives. The email brings the user back to the site to complete the questionaires and read the results.

Chat is a popular way of getting people back to a site – if the experience is likely to be entertaining or informative then it follows that people will want to repeat it. That is part of the theory behind the development of Sony's communicator site W.ear, designed to promote a range of headphones (see case study). Chatters can send an e-flyer to friends, branded with the site's details, to prompt them to get involved and get back to the site.

In its bid to keep users in contact with its web site and build on the relationship that fans have with the Irish boy band Westlife, the record company BMG is truly multi-channelled and contacts teenage fans by text messaging their mobile phones.

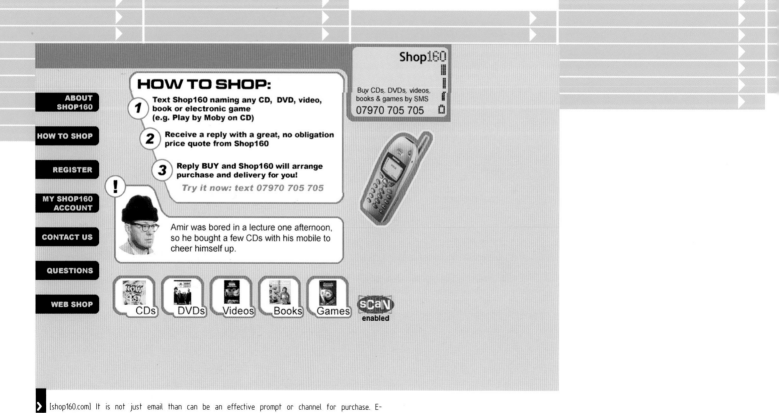

[shop160.com] It is not just email than can be an effective prompt or channel for purchase. E-tailer Shop160 uses SMS text messages, sent to mobile phones to communicate with its customers, alerting them to the availability of products they may want to buy. Users can then return to the site for more information or simply make the purchase by replying to the message with the word 'buy'.

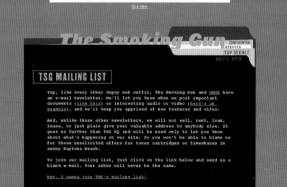

In the latest salvo in the nasty Pam Anderson v. Tommy Lee custody fight, the rock star is seeking "primary physical custody" of the divorced couple's two children because his ex-wife's "judgment is impaired." According to this declaration filed April 9 in Los Angeles Superior Court, Lee claims that Anderson recently filed "frivolous" reports with L.A. child welfare officials alleging "serious misconduct" by Lee. The rock and roll star claimed that Anderson's approach to the Department of Children and Family Services was triggered when the pair's 9-year-old son Brandon was involved in a minor accident at Lee's Malibu home. According to Lee, the child "scraped his face on the side of the Jacuzzi while playing with me." Anderson, Lee contends, is now trying to use this "jacuzzi incident" in a bid to "exclude me from my children based on the unreasonable and irrational view that there is no room for differences of opinion." (5 pages)

Click here for more Anderson v. Lee court documents.

Rx-rated: Tommy Rataen's drug list.

Join TSG's mailing list.

Search The Smoking Gun.

1	**DECLARATION OF TOMMY LEE**
2	
3	I, TOMMY LEE, declare as follows:
4	
5	1. I am the Respondent in the below-entitled action. I have firsthand,
6	personal knowledge of the facts stated herein, and if called as a witness, I could and would

143

[thesmokinggun.com] Like many web sites, thesmokinggun.com allows user to register for an email newsletter alerting them to new content – scandalous and often hilarious documents obtained under the United States' freedom of information laws, in this case. Unlike many other web sites, however, thesmokinggun prominently undertakes not to sell the email address to third parties – unsolicited junk mail or spam now being the main reason that web users are reluctant to give out their contact details.

RESPONDING WITH INTEREST OFFLINE ACTIVITES

A lot of the dotcom businesses that grew up in the venture capital and technology investment bubble, before it burst, were afraid to dabble in offline activities because of fears that they would sully their investment purity. In other words, the value of dotcoms would be compromised by associations with old-fashioned, offline business. Today, with the change in market sentiment, the 'bricks and clicks' model – meaning both an online and offline presence – has become more common. Just as a shop on the street can attract passers-by, it can also prompt people to return to the shop's web site if they view the brand as multi-channelled.

Some online businesses have bought or opened call centres to deal with customer enquiries. Others have found homes with traditional companies and found that the expertise that an offline company has can help the online business grow.

Even for those sites without a counterpart on the offline world, there are a number of offline channels that can be exploited to get users to return. Firebox is an online gadget store. It ensures that it keeps in touch with customers by email but has also invested in its own offline catalogue. In November 2001, it had 175,102 unique visitors. It has 125,000 subscribers to its fortnightly email newsletter and produces 100,000 copies of its printed catalogue.

'Email is the most obvious ways of contacting our customers but once we have their addresses we can go to a whole new level,' explains Firebox's Michael Smith. 'Our offline brochure can then be sent to people.'

Along the same lines, but with an ingenious twist, the site has developed a bespoke set of the cult 70s kids' game Top Trumps. Its version of the card game features gadgets and games for sale on Firebox.com. 'It works as a mini-catalogue. It gives a deeper understanding of the brand and and what we are doing,' Smith says. 'We distribute it primarily to past customers and include one copy in with every parcel we ship out. In November and December 2001 we shipped out approximately 20,000 parcels.'

[mykindaplace.com] The teenage users of mykindaplace.com can order a free printed magalog – a magazine/catalogue hybrid – containing fashion and gift ideas.

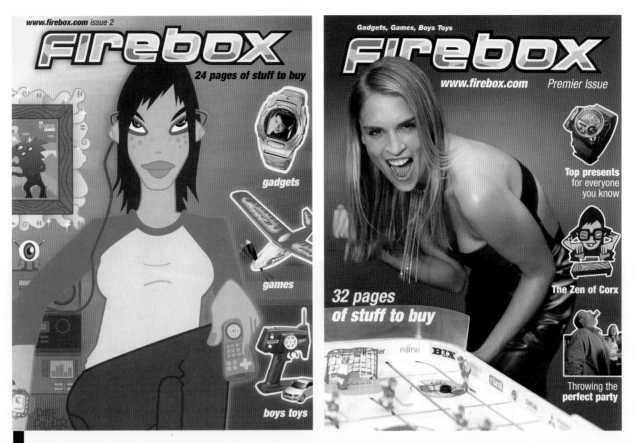

> [firebox.com] Boys' toys e-tailer Firebox.com communicates with its customers offline using a variety of means, including catalogues of its inventory (above) and its bespoke version of the popular 70s game Top Trumps (below) which also acts as a condensed catalogue.

145

RESPONDING WITH INTEREST USER INTEREST

Of course, generating return visits is not just about asking users to come back to a site, which like the other aspects of this chapter relies on prompts and reminders. It is also about making the user want to come back to the site and helping them develop a routine.

In the quest for 'stickiness' – the ability to make users stick around online or return at a later date – content itself is the key factor. For the 2002 World Cup, sportswear brand Umbro launched a site with a tongue-in-cheek quality. It was aimed at those English fans who might have been tempted to dodge work in order to see games on the TV that had early kick-off times. The site included excuses for not going in to work, message forums and, of course, information on the games themselves. With news and TV schedules, the site was a resource to be used regularly before the commencement of the World Cup and throughout its duration. By creating a site that had content designed to be viewed more than once, Umbro ensured that users were regularly reminded of an association between its brand and the World Cup.

> [umbro.com] Users connected to the bunkoff micro site directly or via the main Umbro site.

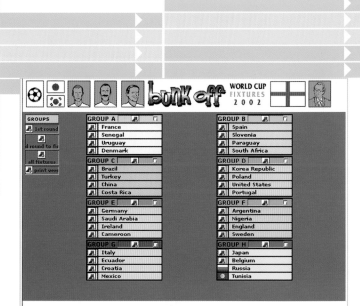

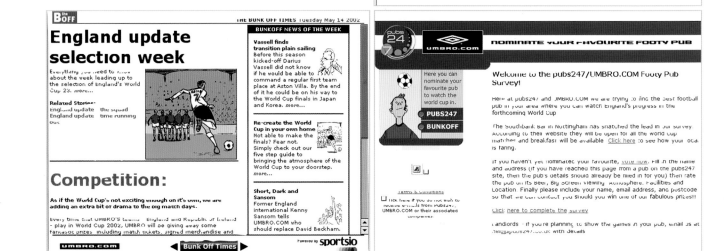

[bunkoff.com] To coincide with the 2002 World Cup, a tongue-in-cheek web site called Bunk Off was launched as an adjunct to the main site of sportswear manufacturer Umbro (umbro.com). Bunkoff.com was targetted at those who might be tempted to take some unauthorised absence from work during the tournament, although was just as useful to those wanting to catch up on developments from their desk. As well as spoof sick notes and the like, the site featured TV schedules, news and results, and details of upcoming fixtures.

FOR SOCIAL SECURITY AND STATUTORY SICK PAY PURPOSES ONLY

<u>NOTES TO PATIENT ABOUT USING THIS FORM</u>

You can use this form either:

    1.   For Statutory Sick Pay (SSP) purposes - fill in Part A overleaf. Also fill in Part B if the doctor has given you a date to resume work. Give or send the completed form to your employer.

    2.   For Social Security purposes -
To continue a claim for state benefit fill in Parts A and C of the form overleaf. Also fill in Part B if the doctor has given you a date to resume work. Sign and date the form and give or send it your Local Social Security Office QUICKLY to avoid losing benefit.

NOTE: To start your claim for State benefit you must use form SC1 if you are self-employed, unemployed or non-employed OR form SSP1 if you are an employee. For further details get leaflet IB202 (from Social Security Local Offices).

Doctor's Stater

In confidence to
Mr/Mrs/Miss/Ms ....
I examined you today/yesterday and advised you that
(a) You need not   (b) you should refrain from work
     refrain from
     work   for*† ....

                OR until ....

147

England update

UMBRO.COM reveals all you need to know about the comings and goings of the England squad this week. Find out who has been staking a claim for contention, who has been shooting themself in the foot and where Sven-Goran Eriksson has been watching football.

more...

Competition:

As if the world cup's not exciting enough on its own, we are adding an extra bit of drama to the big match days.

Every time that UMBRO'S teams — England and Republic of Ireland play in World Cup 2002, UMBRO will be giving away some fantastic prizes, including premier league match tickets, signed merchandise and UMBRO gear.

BUNKOFF NEWS OF THE WEEK

Re-create the world Cup in your own home
Not able to make the finals? Fear not. Simply check out our five step guide to bringing the atmosphere of the world Cup to your doorstep.
more...

Short, Dark and Sansom
Former England international Kenny Sansom tells UMBRO.COM who should replace David Beckham.
more...

Our man in Japan
Former Tottenham Hotspur star Steve Perryman — now a manager in Japan's J.League — writes exclusively for UMBRO.COM. He assesses England's draw for next year's World Cup which takes place in his adopted

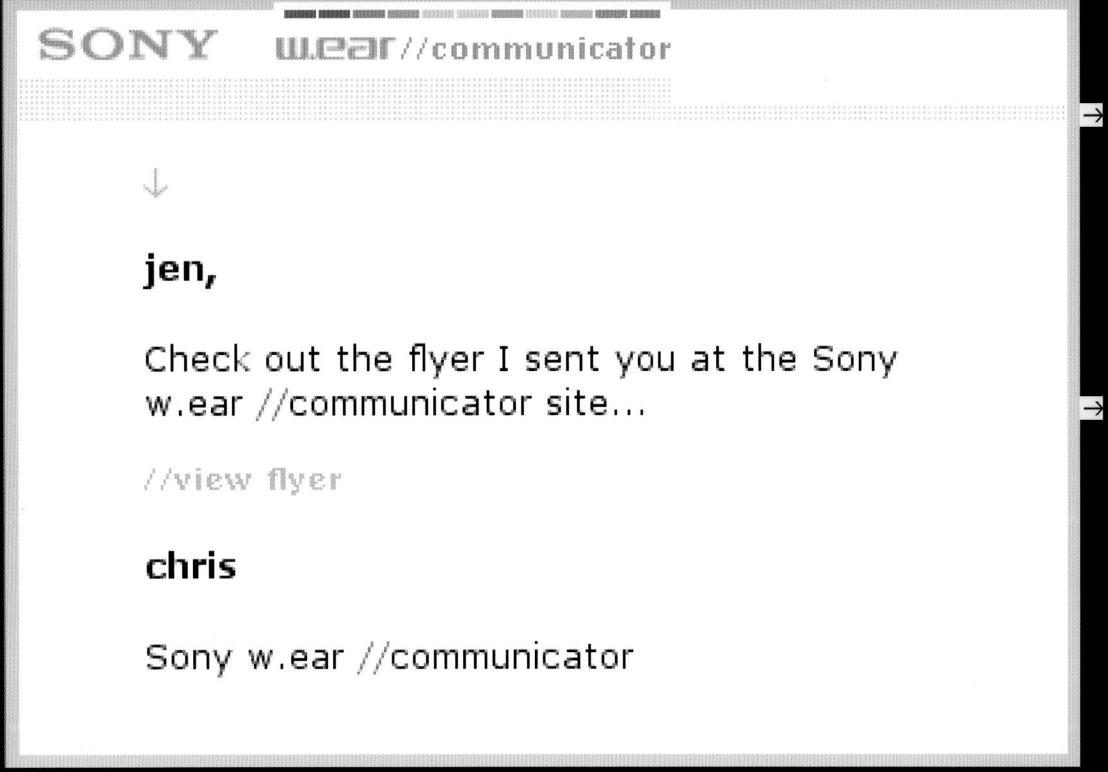

↓

jen,

Check out the flyer I sent you at the Sony
w.ear //communicator site...

//view flyer

chris

Sony w.ear //communicator

→ Invitation email sent via the communicator site.

To promote its new Sony w.ear range of headphones, Sony wanted to build a web site. This posed two challenges. The first was to promote the product while being entertaining enough to interact with customers and potential buyers of Sony's products. The second was that, unlike the majority of Sony's electronic goods, from televisions to cam-corders, there was not a large budget for the launch.

In conjunction with UK-based web design agency Get Frank and brand developer A Vision, a simple solution was found to keep users coming back to the site. A form of one-to-one dialogue was introduced and users could send each other a Sony-branded e-flyer via email through the site. Sony refers to it as a 'communicator' rather than simply a web site. Alison Hardwick, design director of Get Frank, explains: 'Text messaging – a form of one-to-one communication – is currently very popular and with an interactive chat function on the site we could tap in to that feeling.'

It also controls the conversation: Sony wanted to be sure that it worked for the brand and, as children formed the bulk of the target audience, the company wanted to be sure that the site would not upset anyone. 'There are quite a lot of issues when you design a forum-type site where messages are left,' says Hardwick. 'Not least, they need to be regularly maintained.'

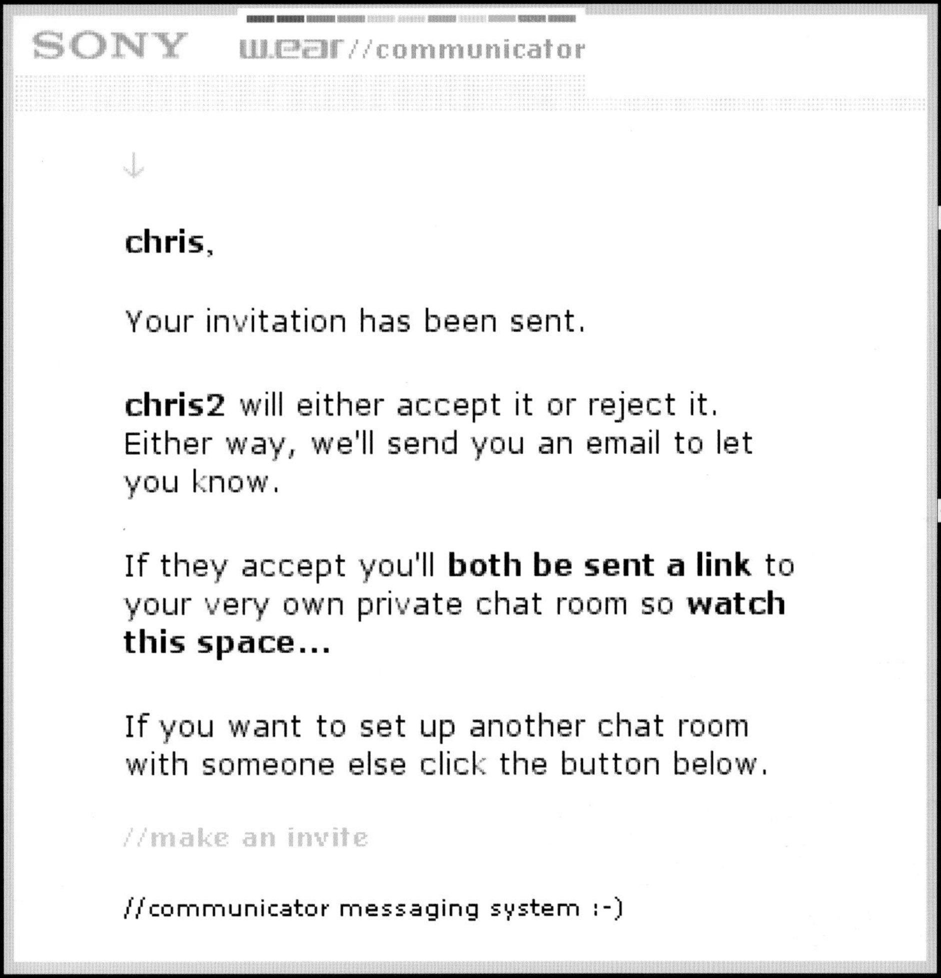

↓

SONY   w.ear//communicator

chris,

Your invitation has been sent.

chris2 will either accept it or reject it.
Either way, we'll send you an email to let
you know.

If they accept you'll **both be sent a link** to
your very own private chat room so **watch
this space...**

If you want to set up another chat room
with someone else click the button below.

//make an invite

//communicator messaging system :-)

→ Confirmation email sent out to the original sender.

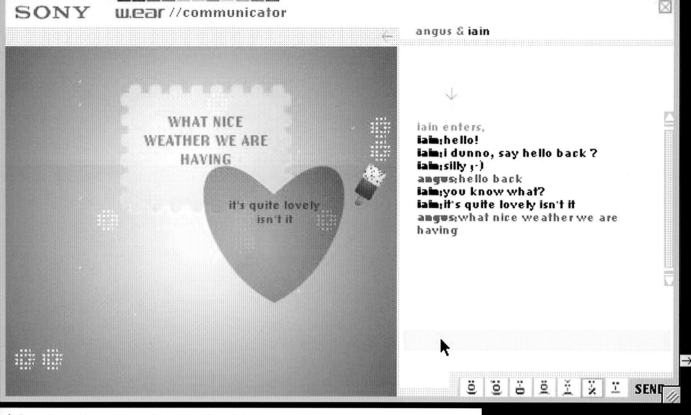

→ Dynamic graphic content supplements text-based chat.

→ Downloads and competitions also feature on the site.

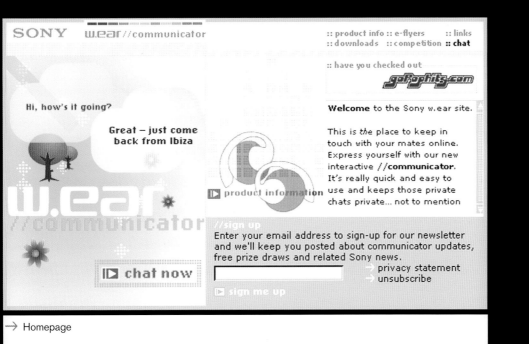

→ Homepage

The headphones come in a range of colours, designed to match the mood of the user, from happy to sad, cheeky to angry. Icons on the site connected with that and the private chat room for each conversation actually changes as the dialogue develops.

Sounds, new colours and icons can all be introduced as the chat continues. A flaming, or angry message can be accompanied by a suitably angry noise, triggered by the user. Although there is naturally a section giving information on the Sony product line, the most important aspect of the site according to Hardwick was the message and sense of community. 'You can go and chat to your friend on the site and send out invites to people to join in and it keeps spreading interest in the site,' Hardwick adds.

05

CONCLUSION

CONCLUSION

So having illustrated and explained the range of factors that influence the design of sites and their methods of getting and retaining an audience, it's clear that nothing is straightforward. There are some obvious conflicts.

Someone wise once said that the only constant is change. For web sites, the only prescription to cope with change is flexibility. A business that is moving into different markets and is under pressure to develop multiple revenue streams, will find it harder to keep its web site simple and straightforward. Good design should allow for the constant pressures of change on web sites while giving them a solid, dependable identity and ensuring that they are navigable and clear.

The community site run from someone's bedroom, the e-tailer and the consumer-facing corporate online brochure face different pressures, and their users have different needs, but none will be effective if the function of the site is impeded by its form.

More usefully, it is perhaps better to understand that users are changing and that sites must reflect their own needs. Bluewave's Dagny Pieto sees a cultural difference in what users look for from a web site on both sides of the Atlantic. This is reflected in the length of time that the Internet has been a mass market proposition and other infrastructure considerations. For instance, in the USA broadband is more of a mass market reality than in Europe. American users also have got used to paying for unmetered access.

From her perspective, working for a European agency in New York, Pieto notes that 'European web design tends to be more techy on the surface, with more flicker and lines. I think the difference lies in that fact that the European web audience is smaller and still consists of a computer elite, while the American audience is a much broader segment of the population. The European computer elite likes the techy edge, while the ordinary American web user would rather keep the technology out of sight. The American Web

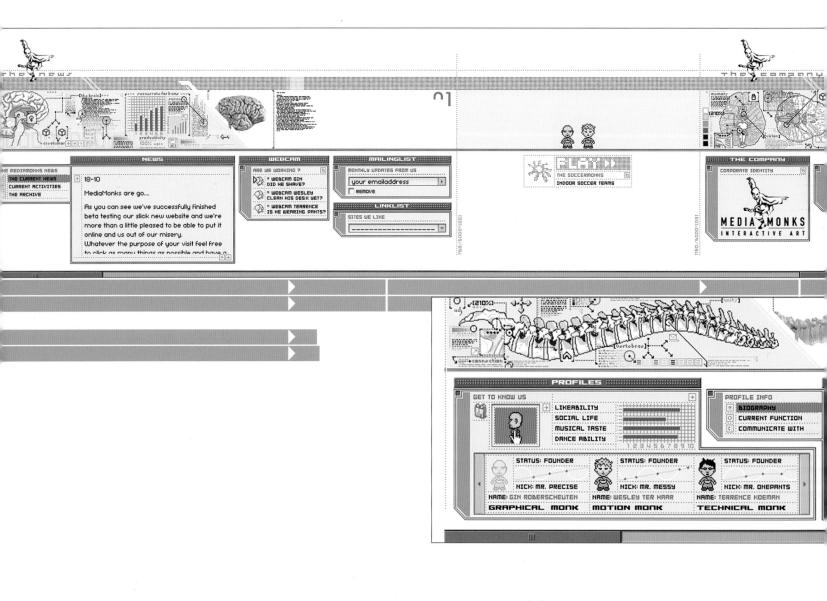

user wants to get things done without having to deal with any "scary technology," while the European user likes to interact with the gadgetry. Hence we get a bigger push to create sites that are accessible to anyone here on this side of the pond.'

This might change as more people come online in Europe and the prospect of broadband as a mass market proposition becomes more and more likely. However, other changes may dictate user preferences. Europeans learnt a bitter lesson with the hype and anti-climactic reality of the Wireless Application Protocol (WAP), which was billed as the Internet on a mobile phone by many who glossed over its weaknesses as a platform and ignored its strengths. How any developments in the progress and use of interactive television and 3G, for example, might affect our demands from the web is still unclear.

However, no matter how relatively sophisticated the US market may appear, American sites and online businesses, like all others around the world, are still learning to survive and adapt. It's a cliché to talk in terms of Internet-time and one that, hopefully, has gone out of vogue in recent years but the simple fact is that the web, as a communication channel and, even more so, as a conduit for business, has had to grow up quickly. Even Google, the search engine that is regularly held up as an exemplar of minimalist and functional web design, has changed in order to develop its revenues. It sells text links on the right hand side of the home page. In this context, it is not such a big change for the user but if both the advertisers and Google are kept happy then it could be a key difference to the bottom line.

Much of this book is concerned with getting more people to come to a web site, and sites are always keen to get as big an audience as possible. But the key to success is getting the right audience. The picture of the user must be in the mind of the designer throughout. Alasdair Scott, creative director of Arnold Interactive, explains that his personal five rules of design include a

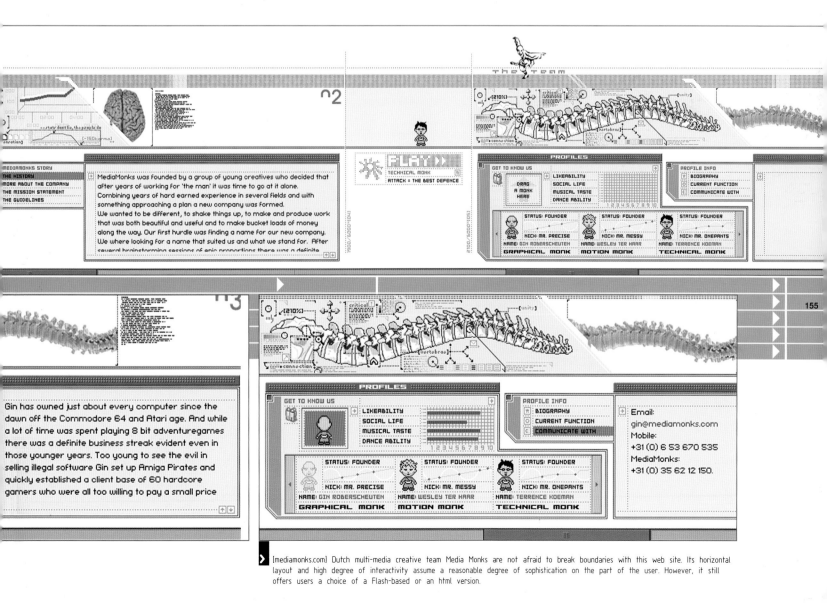

155

[mediamonks.com] Dutch multi-media creative team Media Monks are not afraid to break boundaries with this web site. Its horizontal layout and high degree of interactivity assume a reasonable degree of sophistication on the part of the user. However, it still offers users a choice of a Flash-based or an html version.

CONCLUSION

commitment to compatibility with other channels of communication, and to be realistic – that is to say, not to design sites that needs the latest technology to view for an audience that won't appreciate it.

On the industry commentary web site New Media Knowledge, Zaid Hassan identified 'Moscow Rules Design' as 'one size fits all navigation, the one language fits all content – dictated by the central office, dictated by Moscow, resulting in Moscow rules design'. The examples given in this book are not intended to be the basis of any Moscow Rules, but rather, to illustrate the variety of ways in which the owners and designers of successful web sites have addressed common problems. The myriad considerations involved in solving those problems result in the enormous diversity which is the defining characteristic of the web.

> [pinholespy.com] Designed by Mod7, which prides itself on empathising with its audience, this site aims to teach children how to build their own pinhole camera. Through use of Flash, music, and a storyline based around spy culture, the designers succeeded in creating an educational site which does not patronise its young audience.

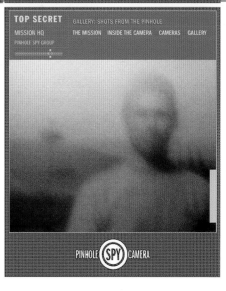

ACKNOWLEDGEMENTS

Thank you to all those who have built, designed and worked on the web sites, digital ideas and businesses mentioned in this book and inspired new thought, and to all those who help(ed) and inspire(d): Scott King and all at Bluewave; Alasdair Scott at Arnold Interactive; Giles Colborne at Euro RSCG Circle; Amanda Anthony and Geoff Sutton at MSN; Damien and Luke at Sports.com; Dave Ward and Douglas McCabe at Fish4; Nicky Iapino and Fiona Yates at Commission Junction; Jon Gisby at Freeserve; Chris Cleave at Lastminute.com; Steve Pankhurst at Friends Reunited; KDD and Lateral's Jon Bains; BMG; Kjell at Firm; Felix Velarde; Bruce Thomas; Steve at Midnight; Firebox's Michael Smith and Andy Smith; Xav Adam; Dr Dan Brown; Christian Guthier at Hi2; Hallam Smallpiece and Jakob Nielsen

To the editors at RotoVision for ideas, know-how and the 'extra mile', and to the designers at bark for a fine job.

And to family and friends including the Revolution team and more people than I can mention at Haymarket Publishing, but, especially, Jane Macken, Vicky Browning and Dominic Mills. To Michael and Sarah for advice and support. My mother and father for everything.

Two dedications: the Future and Grace

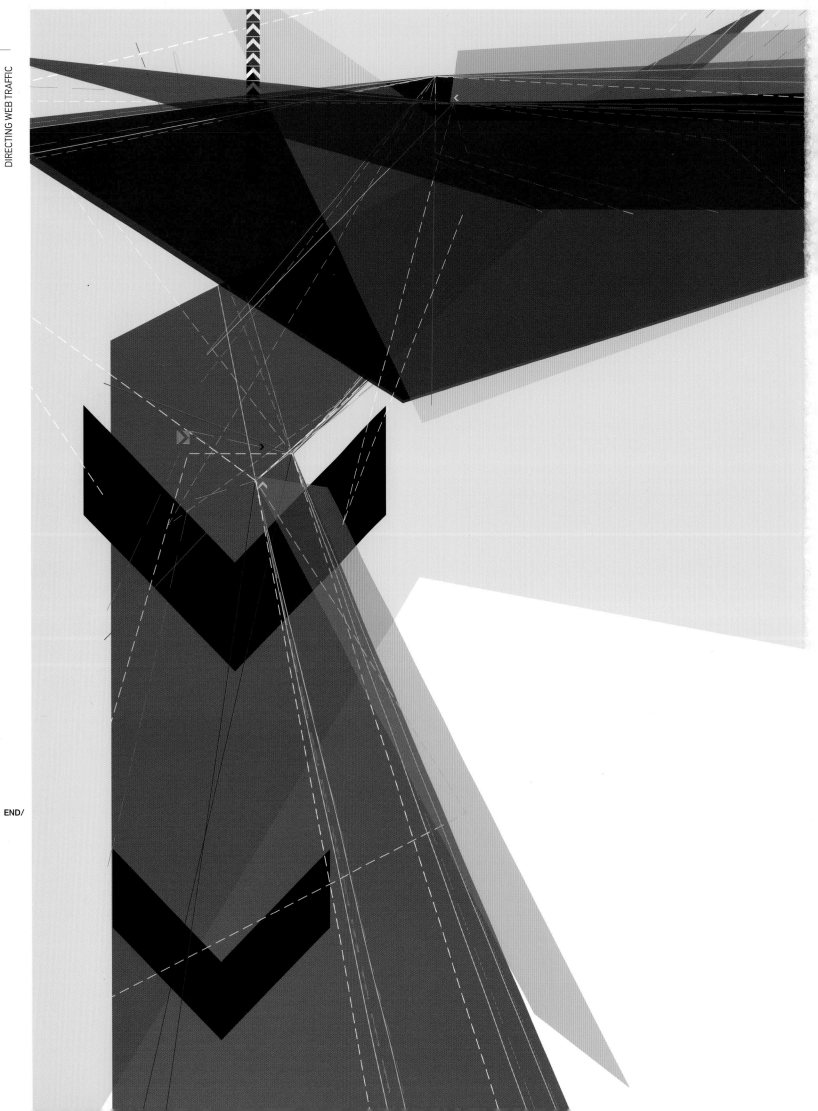

END/